T0196562

DESTINY'S GARDEN

Grab that gift!

Christiana T. Moronfolu

Order this book online at www.trafford.com
or email orders@trafford.com

Most Trafford titles are also available at major online book retailers.

© Copyright 2012 Christiana .T. Moronfolu.

COVER DESIGN BY
TBIC
Batonoflove_ventures@yahoo.com

TYPE SETTING BY
Trafford Publishers

BIBLE REFERENCE
New King James Version (NKJV)

REVISED STANDARD VERSION
COPYRIGHT © 1971 BY COLLINS BIBLE

The bible quotations are from Ilumina DVD.

All rights reserved. No part of this publication may be reproduced, stored in a retrieval system, or transmitted, in any form or by any means, electronic, mechanical, photocopying, recording, or otherwise, without the written prior permission of the author.

Printed in the United States of America.

ISBN: 978-1-4669-4646-0 (sc)
ISBN: 978-1-4669-4645-3 (e)

Trafford rev. 09/25/2012

 www.trafford.com

North America & international
toll-free: 1 888 232 4444 (USA & Canada)
phone: 250 383 6864 • fax: 812 355 4082

1st Corinthians 12 vs. 20

"But now, indeed there are many members, yet one body"

"In Christ there is no east or west
In Him no south or north
But one great fellowship of Love
Through out the whole wide earth"

-William. A . Dunkerly (1908)

CONTENTS

Dedication xi

Acknowledgement xiii

From Me To You xv

PART 1: THE SEED AND THE GARDEN

The Introduction 3

    Grab Your Gift, The Seed 5

    A Physical Gift To You 10

    A Spiritual Gift To You 14

    An Abstract Gift To You 20

    Rise To The Challenge 23

    Seed Adaptability To The Soil 28

    The Physical Boundary 32

    The Spiritual Estate 38

    The Cultural Aura 42

    Overcoming Environmental Challenges 48

PART 2: THE GROWTH AND THE HARVEST

The Introduction 55

    Divine Aid 57

    The Facilitator 61

    The Root Of Destiny 66

    The Shoot For Destiny 72

    The Fruit Of Destiny 76

    Weeding For Destiny 82

    Prunning For Destiny 86

Go Spy The Land. Bring Back The Fruits 91
Reproduce And Replenish 96
Evaluate And Validate Your Product 100
Packaging And Branding 109

PART 3: THE MARKET AND THE BLESSING
Marketing Your Service 115
Your Fallow Season 125
Your Future Market 129
The Cheaper Way For Staying In Business 135
Thanking The Lord Of The Harvest 142
Look Out For The Garden Watchers 145
Look Out For Your Brethren 149
Monopoly 153
Alas! The Competitors 158

Conclusion: Do Not Become God! 163
From Me To You 169

DEDICATION:

To God almighty and Father of our Lord and saviour, Jesus Christ. Thank you for being the enabler of humanity.

Without you, no man can lift his head, but with you, man can face any challenge and still hold his head up high.

ACKNOWLEDGEMENT:

With sincere gratitude and appreciation:

- *To my parents, my siblings and their spouses and all the children: I say thank you for providing the foundational support that helped me grow into all God has for me. You made me believe in myself and appreciate all God have done in my life. The word of God from your mouths has kept me standing tall, after the numerous trials and storms. I would never forget the love God allowed you to show me.*
- *To all ministers of God, who labour in His vineyard, to ensure that we get the finest of the wheat, I say a big thank you to you. Thank you for your obedience to God's word, and thank you for looking after God's children. Like the rod of Moses (backed by the word of God), it is amazing what a sermon directed by God can do. Thank you for all your life-transforming and healing sermons.*
- *To all my mentors in the market place and all those who love to see others succeed the way God wants them to, I say thank*

you. You make the difference in the kingdom of God. You were the ones I saw and made up my mind to always seek God in all I do. You showed me what was possible if I can dare to pursue my God in the market place. Your hands would never lack the support from God in Jesus' name.

- *To all my other good friends, colleagues and family members. I do not think I could have succeeded without God bringing me into your lives. I saw the hand of God in you, and knew that I was fortunate to have come into your lives. Thank you for the race you have run with me and we thank God for the tracks that lie ahead of us. It has been challenging, but enjoyable. We thank God for the sweet fellowship we enjoy in the presence of the Holy Spirit. Thank you for all your love and support in the journey so far.*

From Me To You

Proverbs 18:16 *"A man's gift makes room for him and brings him before great men".*

Have you ever stood before kings?
Would you like to stand before kings?
Do you have what it takes to stand before kings?
Are you prepared to stand before kings?
Do you know that you can stand before kings?

What do you do naturally without supervision?
What can you do without having to put in so much?
What would you do for others, even if you were not paid?
All these are indicators of your gift from God.

Have you discovered your gift?
Do you think it is too small for God to use?
Are you prepared to harness the little God has placed in your hands?
There is a price to pay, to stand before the King.

However small your gifts, how do you intend to multiply it?
Do you squander it because you think it is so small and irrelevant?
Do you ignore it because you think that no one cares?
Perhaps, no one would care until they see you in front of the king.

So why not begin to prepare for the king's presence!

PART 1:
The Seed And The Garden

 Matthew 24 vs. 46-47 *"Blessed is that servant whom his master, when he comes, will find so doing. Assuredly, I say to you that he will make him ruler over all his goods"*.

DIVERSITY

Romans 12 vs. 6 *"Having then gifts differing according to the grace that is given to us, let us use them: if prophecy let us prophesy in proportion to our faith"*.

The Introduction

Matthew 11 vs. 12 *"And from the days of John the Baptist until now the kingdom of heaven suffers violence, and the violent take it by force".*

This part deals with practical ways of how you can discover your gift, develop it and market it, so it can be of benefit to you and your sphere of influence. Violently taking what is yours is a forceful charge that is synonymous with grabbing. So what is grabbing?

Grabbing is a militant and an assertive word, which suggests aggressively taking ownership or responsibility for something. Taking ownership of your life would therefore require you taking responsibility for your location (physical, spiritual, emotional, mental, social, financial, e.t.c), experience (past, present and future), and gifts (physical, spiritual and abstract). Once you begin to do this, the bible says that life would open doors of opportunities for you. Your life is a garden and you.

You need to grab your garden from the hands of the devourers—worthless living. Your garden is where your destiny (fate) can be determined. This comes with a fight, so I challenge you today, take charge. Grab your life today. Harness your gift now. Begin to deploy it. You must and would have a glorious fate, in Jesus' name.

Grab Your Gift, The Seed

1

Ecclesiastes 3 vs. 13 *"and also that every man should eat and drink and enjoy the good of all his labor – it is the gift of God"*.

We have identified God; as the source of all gifts and abilities. He is also the one who blesses man (enables him to prosper) and gives him abilities in the form of gifts. So what is a gift? A gift may be defined as an aid, contribution or offering given to a person. As an aid, it helps the person perform a task or an assignment better. As a contribution, it helps improve the quality and quantity of the person's desired outcome. As an offering, it is given as a reward for an acceptable behaviour, position, or event. Whichever way you choose to look at it, a gift carries a positive connotation. It is given to enrich your garden-(life). James 1 verse 17.

Everyone has a seed to sow or a gift with which to make a positive impact, but not every one has been able to use their gift to produce outstanding works. In the bible, Moses was an example of a man that had an ordinary rod. Before Exodus 3, nothing was said of him. On his first encounter with God, all that was in his hand was a rod. Left to him, all he could see was the rod in the hands of a murderer on the run! However, God wanted to change his story, he wanted his garden to turn out beautiful. God wanted Moses to have a glorious destiny. The God who met Moses that day has now come to meet with you. Exodus 4 vs. 10-12.

> Everyone has a seed to sow or a gift with which to make a positive impact

However, God who can make little with much transformed his rod from an ordinary rod to a rod that performed signs and wonders throughout his lifetime. The rod became a seed that God used to deliver Israel from bondage. His gift to you is the seed He has placed in your hands.

What is it that you have in your possession? What ever you love to do that can add value to your life and the lives of those around you, is your seed, which can become a gift. It does not matter if you think it is irrelevant or common. If it has the potential to improve the quality of life, it is from God, and it is worth harnessing (nurturing to maturity). Give yourself the opportunity to try.

The process of identifying, developing, and deploying your gift could be compared to the manner in which a seed is harnessed, in order to bring about a harvest. Once the seed is sown, and conditions are right, it would yield a harvest. In talking about the seed, there is the potent seed (those things you do so well that it is obvious to every one around you) and the latent seed (those things you can do well, but are not very obvious). I used to think that I did not have any gift until the Holy Spirit used the chessboard to explain the potent and latent seed to me.

On the chessboard, you control your players, and move them according to their abilities. Some can only move one-step forward or back ward. Some are allowed to move sideways, while some are allowed to move in a diagonal form. There are still some that are able to move in all directions, these are the more powerful players on the board. Now to play the game of chess and legally remain in the game, you must comply by its rules.

In the garden of destiny (life), you are in control of the seed God places in your hands. You may choose to develop it or allow it to die. God has given you the power to develop His gifts in you. Napoleon, one of the great minds of old once said, *"What you are is God's gift to you, what you make of yourself, is your gift to God"*.

More so, like the game of chess, the players represent the resources *(seed)* in your life (garden). There are some talents that should be developed now *(players that can move in any direction)* because they are relevant now. Whichever way they turn, they would yield increase, so discover them, and begin to move them around. Some could move one-step forward, representing the talents that need a little bit of effort to convert then into wealth. For those players that can move backward or side ways, they represent the talents that although present, can wait, until the opportune time, when it would be relevant. You must follow the directions of the manual to play and win legally. The same rules apply if your life would ultimately be referred to as "a well watered garden".

Like wise, as a seed coat covers the seed, so is your gift hidden inside you. In order words, God has already given you the seed that can turn to a gift. Both within and around the garden are diverse seeds waiting to be planted. As you mature, you ought to know the type of flowers to enrich your garden with, and this would determine what seeds you would cultivate. Remember knowing this is not enough, you also need the help of God; the one who can empower you to cultivate. 2nd Corinthians 4 vs. 7

Any gift that would turn to a seed in your garden is what you like. This is what you would persist in doing even if you are not making money.

In addition, exposure to various activities (even it means helping people) can help spot this. Study what they do and see if you like it. My mum used to tell us while we were growing up that when we help people, we were invariably helping ourselves. In my early years, needlework was part of the activities I got involved with at school. Knowing you can produce things at a tender age was great knowledge. For me, threading the needle was not. Although my mum loved sewing, and I occasionally helped her thread the needle. I could not honestly say that being a dress maker was a hobby.

She said her grand ma was a successful tailor. I admire people who work with fabrics, because it requires a lot of creativity and high intelligence to come up with designs, and turn the plain fabrics into different styles of clothing. I discovered that I did not get my kicks from it. The activity was over taken by much more colourful ones. There were events from two realms, which constantly pre occupied my life; when there was no one around the public—dancing and singing, the other was working with colourful images. Writing in my early years yielded very good grades, yet I did not know I could convert it to commercial gain.

Colours just make me thrilled. What I did in private was good, as I got personal fulfilment and joy there. I later discovered that that to get the full benefits of the fulfilment, however, it must be shared with the public.

In addition, whatever will generate money for you must be linked with what the public will accept. You know where you get your kicks from, so you need to look for a way to translate your private acts into public acts that would bring fulfilment your way; when shared. When God gave the Israelites the promised land—as a gift, they were instructed to work on it. God left you and I with the responsibility for prospering our garden. Joshua 1 vs. 8. The anxieties I had just before leaving secondary education were numerous, it aggravated just before I graduated from college. The only thing I knew was that I could not afford to fail. In my worries, I got a visitation from God, and the Holy Spirit asked me *"What is in your hand"*? I looked at my hands and did not reply. As far as I was concerned, there was nothing there. He later on went on to tell me *"your gift is in your mouth"*. I needed to open it and pray; commanding my hands to begin to work for me.

Therefore, if you are like me, go to God and prayerfully ask Him what He is going to bless in your garden, so you can have a glorious destiny. There are diverse gifts in the world. In this book, I have classified them under three categories; the physical, the spiritual and the abstract. You can grab any of these. You can transform it into seed. You can use it to enrich your garden.

A Physical Gift To You

Zechariah 8 vs. 12 *"For the seed shall be prosperous; the vine shall give her fruit, and the ground shall give her increase, and the heavens shall give their dew; and I will cause the remnant of this people to possess all these things".*

This talks about a three dimensional blessing; from the ground, the field or garden and the heavens; a multi-dimensional blessings of God in your garden. It is not restricted. The outpouring of His blessings takes care of everything in your garden. Before the blessings can be of benefit to you, however, there might be some things you need to do, and some discoveries you need to make concerning yourself. The first is discovering your physical gift and putting it to work.

In your life, there is always something to do that has the potentials of producing a harvest. How healthy your seed grows is determined by how much effort is put into it. Your physical gifts therefore include finance, abilities, experience, skills, good health, positive attitudes, service, e.t.c.

Considering the physical gift in your life involves taking responsibility for, and identifying the things you do naturally, developing and deploying them for the betterment of those around you. The advantage of this can never be overemphasized. By taking ownership for your gifts, you can save those around you as well. This is one of the ways of commanding the attention of men of influence; whom having being blessed by you, can help push you further than you ever imagined. Proverbs 22 vs. 29.

The physical work that excels would promote you. The art of building was a skill Noah had in the bible. It was a seed in his garden of destiny. When called by God, he was able to take up the responsibility of building the Ark. Genesis 6 vs. 22.

You should also be able to discern the timing of God for the season. This helps you know what to do at the right time. An example is a gardener that uses his discretion to know when to water his garden and in what quantity. Noah displayed this principle in that he knew that the One who led them into the ark (*in His time)*, will also lead them out (*in His time*). He understood that nothing happens outside God's timing. Genesis 7 vs. 4.

More so, in considering the physical seed in your garden of destiny, you must possess the tenacity to wait on God regardless of what the circumstances (emotional, mental, health wise, financial, e.t.c) around you say. It is just like how every farmer learns to discern the timing between the seed and the harvest. Even when it was obvious that the waters were abated, Noah waited for God to signal his release. He was not disappointed, because the bible records in Genesis 8 vs. 1 *"God remembered Noah"*.

More so, the same flood (challenge) that destroyed humanity was the same flood that lifted and sustained Noah and his company. The challenges that would destroy the world could be the very thing that God would use to elevate you, if only you would co-operate with Him. Genesis 8 verse 10-12, *Genesis 8 verse 15*

For me, my short attention span in the classroom many years ago meant that I was shut in and locked up in my own world. The stories I processed in mind as I observed my environment were very positive and ideal, and

> You should also be able to discern the timing of God for the season.

they had positive influence on my outlook. I was very good in composition then. Storey telling was a favourite pass time.

However, you would agree with me that it was the contender of my mind, as those stories kept me out of time and reality. I realised that for me to excel the way I wanted, I needed to get back in time. I battled with this for almost twenty years. The more I battled with this, the more attacks I had in my sleep. Under the guidance of God, I was able to develop the art of learning properly, concentrating well and living in time. This was possible through intensive training, as i exposed myself to the different personal development programmes available, Christian seminars and preaching, studying the bible personally, praying and fasting. By the time, I got to the university after my college degree in architecture, things improved. It was at this point that I decided to develop my writing skill. God encouraged me not to look down on it.

The God that remembered Noah and brought him out of the ark, remembered me, and can remember you. Therefore, if you feel shut in today, you too can cry out to God to remember you.

Finally, thanksgiving puts a seal on your seed, as you put it to work. Thanking God as the seed goes into the ground is putting the angels of God who are your ministering spirits to work. As soon as Noah and his family got out of the ark, realising the great deliverance God had wrought for them, he offered a sacrifice of thanksgiving (seed) to God. Genesis 8 verse 20-22. What was the significance of this? Prior to Noah's offering, God had cursed the ground because of the wickedness of man, but as soon as Noah offered a sweet sacrifice to God, God vowed never again to curse the ground, regardless of what man did. What this means is that when you sow a seed, you are sure to reap its harvest, all conditions being satisfied.

Today I encourage you, touch the loving nature of God. Provoke an everlasting covenant with Him for your seed. Enjoy the privilege of collaborating with God through your seed.

A Spiritual Gift To You

Isaiah 44 vs. 3 *"For I will pour water upon him that is thirsty, and floods upon the dry ground: I will pour my spirit upon thy seed and my blessing upon thine offspring"*

From the previous chapter, we saw how Noah considered his building skills, which is a physical gift and how it was used to save his family and preserve God's other creations. This would not have been possible if he had not taken charge of his spiritual gift (righteousness — walk with God). Spiritual seed is only available and put to maximum use in God. Your spiritual gift is therefore what you get by aligning yourself with the word of God (His instructions and blessings). It is what God gives you to aid your walk with Him. It also helps others in their walk with Him.

The reward of this type of seed is amazing. God is the one who can plant this seed in your garden, not you. No matter how hard you try, unless He plants them in your garden, you cannot lay hold of them. When he plants them, prosperity is inevitable. Does this mean that there are some gardens that do not have them? Yes.

These are the ones that have not asked for His presence. They believe that their presence is sufficient. In these gardens, there is no sign of increase. How ever; as you long for His presence, He is able to sow spiritual gifts in you. Pursue Him. 1st Corinthians 14 vs. 1. A man who pursues spiritual gift is one who is prepared to take ownership of his walk with God. The bible records that Lot was a righteous man. While Noah was able to influence and save his entire household, Lot was not. His sons—law were destroyed. May be he had some character flaws in his garden of destiny that he refused to address (greed, folly and laziness). This assumption is based on the following premises:

> God is the one who can plant this seed in your garden, not you.

> ➤ Greed: We are told that his choice of Sodom and Gomorrah was based on a wrong motive.
> ➤ Folly: We are told that his sons-in-law mocked him, when he attempted to proclaim the word of God to them. They were not used to Lot the preacher! They knew him as their father in law, not a preacher!

> ➤ Laziness: We are told that when he was instructed to flee to the mountains, he chose to settle in the valley.

Remember, the fact that you have embraced your spiritual gift does not mean that you can influence others with it. Look at Lot. You still need to take it a step further and process it in a way that would positively have impact others. 1st Corinthians 12 vs. 1. God's intention is to save everyone in your sphere of influence, but He may be waiting on you to show them the way through your words and deeds. To possess your spiritual gift, you must be responsible for your walk with God in your garden of destiny. How do you walk with God?

I illustrated an example in the previous chapter when I described how God was able to help me with my attention deficiency in the classroom. You need to desire for the Holy Spirit to come in. You need to be prepared to follow his leading. His leading does not go beyond the word (the bible). Pray and study the word. Fellowship with the brethren in church. Study to show yourself diligent before God (not man) in whatever you do. The exam of man is periodical, God's exam continues on a second by second basis. Whoever passes man's exam and fails God's would end up a frustrated and failed individual. God does not want to advertise failure, He wants to advertise you. What can He use through you to demonstrate His power in the world?

As earlier explained, the manifestation of a well-watered garden is a healthy and beautiful environment. The manifestation of your walk with God would produce the required result you need for a successful life. 1st Corinthians 12 vs. 7-10. A successful spiritual walk would be characterised by:

➢ Utterance of wisdom—This gift, if properly harnessed can bring you tremendous wealth. It refers to being able to release sound words for every situation. Like King Solomon, people you do not know would begin to look for you. They would want to hear you speak, because your words would be full of life (health, wealth, and hope). It would enrich your garden and inspire others to begin to cultivate their gardens as well. Proverbs 22 vs. 11 *"He who loves purity of heart and has grace on his lips, the king will be his friend"*.

➢ Utterance of knowledge—This is a useful seed (tool) in soul winning and for persuading people into taking an action. At times, all it takes for a person to believe in God is for God to reveal certain truths about them to you. God can also the solution to a problem (national or international) to you. This is what He did for Joseph. In his garden, Joseph had a gift of interpretation of dreams and utterance of knowledge. He used this to deliver Egypt from famine.

➢ Faith—By choosing to develop your seed of faith, you can save your circle of influence and align yourself for destiny. Rehab is a classic example of someone who caught this revelation and applied it. Tending well to your garden influences others as well. Hebrews 11 vs. 31 *"By faith the harlot Rahab did not perish with those who did not believe, when she had received the spies with peace"*.

➢ Gift of healing—When you develop this seed, you would be able to bring joy, peace, and progress, to any circle you find yourself. Imagine what tremendous joy you would bring to a family, if God used you to heal one of its members of a terminal disease. Peter and John healed the lame man at the beautiful gate, and brought joy into his life and family. What you deposit into people's lives will eventually come back to you (in multiple folds). Acts 3 vs. 7-8

➤ Working of miracles — This gift comes with boldness to enable you do what you would not do ordinarily. It is useful in soul winning, healing, and deliverance (of any kind). It opens you up to be used by God in unusual ways. Paul was one man who had this gift. Acts 19 vs. 11 *"Now God worked unusual miracles by the hands of Paul"*.

➤ Prophesy — This gift can turn any nasty situation around. These situations could range from famine in a land to bareness in a home. It could also be unfruitfulness at work or dissatisfaction in ones marriage. Whichever form it takes, at the word of the Lord, which is also a seed, it can turn around. In Hannah's moment of grief over her bareness, Eli prophesized fruitfulness to her. This changed her situation and restored her back to herself. 1st Samuel 1 vs. 17-20.

➤ Discerning of spirits — This gift from God can deliver you from fraudsters. You can pave the way to your success and the success of those around you with this gift. It would not be easy for the people to defraud you, as you would be able to tell the spirit that they are operating in. You can also cause revival to occur in a city with this seed. Phillip drove out the demons that were controlling and oppressing people in a city and caused a revival there. Acts 8 vs. 7-10

➢ Various kinds of tongues—This seed is useful in identifying with and persuading people to do things for you. People tend to relax when they feel that you share something in common with them. It is also a useful tool in evangelism. 2nd Timothy 1 vs. 6

In closing, I would say, develop your seed. Let your gift create opportunities for you. Allow your gift to strengthen you for the task ahead.

An Abstract Gift
To You

Ecclesiastes 2 vs. 5 *"I made gardens and parks, filling them with all kinds of fruit trees".*

We have been looking at the diverse gifts that is available to us in life. There are gifts you can hold onto, and some are streamlined for the christian who decides to improve the quality of her life in God. When you think of a gift or seed, what comes to mind immediately are the tangibles; yet the abstract is intangible and cannot be comprehended with the natural senses. It can only be conceived in the mind. An abstract gift is therefore anything the mind can perceive that would improve the quality of life and produce a desired outcome, if brought into reality. Examples of these include visions, ideas, inspirations, and dreams. It is so easy to overlook this seed. 1st Timothy 4 vs. 14.

More so, creating from the abstract started with God in Genesis chapter one. We read that there was darkness *(confusion, chaos, and unfruitfulness)*. As God spoke the word (the seed), in the presence of the spirit, what He said became visible. The Spirit of God intervened *(inspiration; in the form of divine ideas in the mind; bringing the intangible to life)* and what He said became reality.

All through this chapter, we see this line recurring: . . . . *Then God said, "Let there be . . . . and it was so"*. This, as we would later discover, formed the pattern for creating or establishing His purpose all through the bible. If you would be productive as God expects us to be, then you would have to apply the same principles to your garden of destiny daily. It only requires faith. God Almighty spoke in the presence of His spirit, and He saw what He demanded for. This means that we need to create with our mouth what the Spirit of God drops within our spirit (the abstract). Being made in God's image, having a measure of His spirit, all we need is to speak *(in line with the mind of God)*, and the Lord would back our words with evidence.

However, it should be noted that when we speak, we do not need to see to believe. When a gardener plants a seed, he does see it grow immediately, but given the right conditions, growth becomes inevitable. God; the master creator, did not wait to see if that which He said would happen. He spoke, and the circumstances began to align themselves to conform to His word.

God saw that His creation was good, because He had the mind to create good things. The goodness came from the words God spoke.

Further, down the line, on creating man, He charged him with the mandate of continuing the work of creation, seeing that He has already breathed into him. **Job32 vs. 8** *"For it is the spirit in man; the breathe of the almighty that gives him understanding"*.

From creation, God began the art of using the abstract to produce and name things, and immediately He made man; He passed the baton to him. He would have to live with whatever he choose to call the world around him. We also saw how Adam was charged with naming the animals and how he finally named Eve. Your seed or gift would work in the same way. First, it would be conceived in your mind, and then you have to speak it into manifestation.

> God saw that His creation was good, because He had the mind to create good things.

Arise, speak and work out your ideas. Allow heavenly aid to gravitate towards you. Give room to the birthing of what was once an abstract idea.

Rise To The Challenge

Song of Solomon 4 vs. 12 "*You are like a private garden, my treasure, my bride! You are like a spring that no one else can drink from, a fountain of my own.*

By now you must be confident of who your source and sustainer is. Repeatedly, the Lord God assures you of His ability and willingness to be with you, regardless of the circumstance. It doesn't matter how many people are on the earth He says there is room to single you out, and relate with you as an individual, not as a twin, nor a crowd. You are a single entity before God. You must face this fact and take responsibility for your garden. God wants to fellowship with you on a level that no man can compare with. He longs to show you his sovereignty that he may proof Himself as the one to give you pleasure and delight. The ball is in your court and your decision proves how much of this you can experience. Joshua 24 vs. 15

More so, if you would ever take full responsibility for your gift, circle of influence, and environment, you must be prepared to rise up to the challenges as well. Your challenges could range from physical, to emotional (depression, anger, anxiety, e.t.c), financial, mental, and social inadequacies. Depending on how you view it, the challenge could be a seed to secure a better future; which could provoke you until you rise up and become an over comer. I remember the challenges I have faced in life. A chronic one was a spiritual battle I faced for a long time, which came because of an arrow shot at me in 2008. The devil deployed his best weapon of ignorance against me, which left me almost psychologically incapable. *I promised God to concentrate on His praise and go into a personal business with Him*; called "Look to Jesus, Leave The Devil (L2J Ltd)". This was a turbulent period for me, but as I remained under God's guidance, I was able to achieve what I never thought was possible in my entire life. My entire life was re-arranged, looking back now; it was as though God Himself disgraced the devil, because despite the challenge, I was able to accomplish much more than I imagined. I can see the rewards or fruits from that season. The Lord directed my work then. The best way to summarise it is 'a period of replenishment'. Isaiah 61 vs. 8.

For many people, living with a long-term ailment is the last thing they wish for themselves or their family. Yet we live in a world where life throws all sorts of obstacles our way. Some are surmountable, and others are here to challenge our growth in God. For the ones that challenge our growth in God, we would have to quit blaming our circumstances, hold on to the word of God and like Joshua, declare, *"As* for *me and my house, we would serve the Lord"*, irrespective of life's obstacles. If you would pray to God to open your eyes, you would see the numerous gifts and privileges He has assigned to aid your journey through life, irrespective of the obstacles.

In addition, as you rise to your challenges, the result of Psalm 121 would become evident to you. It may be hard, but it promises to be a very joyful one. The benefit of looking to God when you cannot find your way, or when life ceases to have meaning cannot be over emphasized. Like me, if you desire to take charge of your life, take a visit to Psalm121, for the following benefits below.

Firstly, help is released as you dare to look to God. The creator will give you supernatural ideas for breakthrough in every sphere of your life—mental, financial, moral, social, emotion, e.t.c. The help no man can give, God would make available. There is limit to which man can help, but there is no limit with God. Psalm 121 vs. 1-2. He would keep you steadfast and in the face of storms, you would be immoveable and come out victorious in life. You would be able to embrace the challenges that life throws at you and use the obstacles of life as a stepping-stone to your expected end. While some get to their destination half dead, you would get to yours standing tall. The storms of life would not destroy the seed in your garden. Psalm 121 vs. 3.

He would keep His eyes on you all the time and constantly guard your interest, even when you are not around. He would not allow you make the wrong decisions, neither would He allow the enemy to defraud you and even fight for you, when you cannot fight for yourself. Psalm 121 vs. 4.

He is able to keep you in comfort, peace, joy, love, steadfastness so that you can be He wants you to be. The journey could be lonesome at times,

> The help no man can give, God would make available.

but you have this assurance of guidance from God. He is able to keep you from you, from your enemies and your friends. The sole purpose of this is to help you become who He wants you to be. Guess what, every single person goes through this route as well, it is not unique to you. Psalm 121 vs. 5.

More so, in a garden, depending on the season of the year, some trees shed their leaves, and afterwards bring forth fresh ones. There are things that would periodically be shed off to allow the new in your life.. God would shield you from the aftermath of life's challenges on a daily basis. The journey of life takes you through a series of encounters,; positive and negative. These can also be compared to a burning object that leaves behind ashes. Psalm 121 vs. 6

The ashes, can no longer be destroyed by heat. In the same vein, God may allow the circumstances to reduce you to ashes (emotionally, spiritually, health wise, financially, mentally, e.t.c). As long as the ashes are recognizable and still on the ground, they are still useful. You can be preserved from the heat of life, so God can use you. Psalm 121 vs. 7.

He would preserve you when the enemy attacks through sickness, disease, accidents, pre mature deaths, hunger, strive, rebellion, works of the flesh, e.t.c. God keeping you from all these means that you would be shielded from them all. The picture God gave me for this was the bubble wrap. Consider a very fragile parcel that needs to be delivered (moved) from one location to the other. To avoid damaging it, it may be enveloped in bubble wraps to protect it if it drops while handling. As a child of God, in the course of your interactions with man and God, you would be expected be on the move and as the bubble wraps on the fragile parcel, God would shield you from being mismanaged. Psalm 121 vs. 7.

In addition, He would preserve your soul. Which is the seat of your intellect—your thinking, emotions and will. The Lord is able to preserve your thinking, so it does not run amok in the face of challenges. He is also able to preserve your emotions, when the enemy introduces disappointments and pain into your life. Better still, He will preserve your will, so you do not compromise your standards. There is a high price to pay, if you do this. If you ask me, I do not know how I survived the attack since 2008. The lord allowed the devil to attack my mind, but as I held onto His word, they did not prevail. The attack slowed me down, as I had to take my time to filter sound doctrines from the demonic voices I was hearing. Psalm 121 vs. 8.

God would preserve every move you make, so you do not have to be afraid when you travel, take decisions, or make choices. For example, you would know when to move and when not to, where to go and where not to, who to marry and who not to, who to do business with and who not to, who to keep company with and who not to. It was only when I made up my mind to look to God that I received the courage to take ownership of my life. Look to Him today, and grab the courage to take ownership of your garden of destiny. Romans 8 vs. 28.

In conclusion, as you look to Him, He would show and teach you how to take ownership of your life.

It is never too late to start. It is never too late to surrender to Him. It is never too late for God to turn your life around for good.

Seed Adaptability To The Soil

Ezekiel 17:8 *"It was planted in a good soil by great waters, that it might bring forth branches, and that it might bear fruit, that it might be a goodly vine.*

Seed adaptability is how well a seed responds (in growth) to its environmental conditions (the soil). It refers to how well the seed seats in the soil and conditions it self for growth. As earlier described, a seed is anything that can be reproduced. When it positively affects people, it is a good seed, and where there is an adverse effect, it is a bad seed. The soil, depending on its type can hold a structure. Its horizontality or inclined property supports animal movement, and depending on their nature; from loose particles to clay, they can hold vegetation and plantation to the ground. They also offer support for growth and movement.

As long as the support is in good condition, there would be growth at the right time. Growth in your garden of destiny requires the condition of the source and support to be right. We have already identified God as the only true source and support and most times, He works through people. **Psalm 1 vs. 3**
With Him as your source and support, your garden would never lack the necessary nutrients (wisdom, sanctification, e.t.c). I enjoy planting in my spare time. Some years back, I observed how a hard soil was firstly broken up into particles with a shovel, and then mixed with manure. The Holy Spirit then began to minister to me. God has to break people, make them loose (light / flexible), and impact His idea into them (as the manure was being added in bits to the soil), before they can be productive. No matter how good the seed is, if the soil is not loose, air would not be able to circulate well within the particles, and this would invariably impede the growth and beauty of the flowers.

Bearing these in mind, we see that nature and nurture is required for the successful growth of a garden and your life. The different seasons of the year also influences the soil condition. They are determinants for the growth of certain flowers; while some thrive all year round, some blossom only in specific seasons. This is also true of the development of your gifts — the gifts that has been, the gifts that would be and the gift that is. **John 12 vs. 24**

It is not only the soil that needs to be loosened up, the grain or seed must also be broken up to reveal its content (potential). It must die (be broken up). Some gifts may not manifest until certain cultures and traditions are dissected and addressed. In breaking the soil, you would see maggots, fossils, thrash, and other debris in between the particles — these are useful to some people and of no use to others. In the abstract sense loosening up for you may be exposing certain "skeletons in the closet".

This closet could be physical, spiritual, or cultural. There are two purposes for exposing the closet the first is to learn and grow, and the second is to assist others in learning and growing. It is not to punish the people who share the closet with you, but to encourage others in a similar situation to learn and handle theirs. At other times; it may be to bring about genuine repentance, and draw the perpetrators (if there are any) of wrong to God. After all, the Holy Spirit convicts people to bring them to repentance.

2nd Corinthians 7:10

More so, remember this truth, you are not the only one with closets to expose. We all have ours. I am joining my trainers in exposing mine as a response to the Holy Spirit. My method of exposure is not the only one, as there are different kinds of closets. At times, exposing and studying the skeletal frame may be all a medical student needs to understand to fulfil his destiny. So watch how I handle mine, watch how your motivators handled theirs, and girded with this knowledge, you can then decide on how to handle yours.

When you have handled it well in private, God may then decide to allow you handle it in public. It is not always easy, but it is worth it. I never feel bad about sharing my testimony. It is not always comfortable, but I know it blesses and encourages my audience.

However, before you begin to expose your closet to the public, master the skeletons in it, and be comfortable with them, but be determined to get rid of them all costs. (That closet needs to be aired at all times and perfumed with the aroma of Christ). You would need

> That closet needs to be aired at all times and perfumed with the aroma of Christ.

this determination when all the focal rays converge towards you (in public—in the heat of criticisms). Your determination to stand in public will force the required response from people with time—their awareness of their need for help in the area addressed.

If you are not determined, fear would force you to leave the public scene before you get a response from people. Remember, in familiarising yourself with your closet (in your garden of destiny), you may discover a treasure or gift (experience) that can bless your generation and the ones to come.

You can therefore see the need for your soil to be in good condition. You can see the impact of a good seed. You can see the effort required for growth. Adaptability is the word. Congruency is the way. Growth is the goal.

The Physical Boundary

7

Leviticus 25 vs. 19 *"Then the land will yield its fruit, and you will eat your fill, and dwell there in safety".*

The physical boundary of your garden of destiny consists of relationships that enrich it; beginning from having a relationship with yourself, and extending it to your family. In it, God gave you the gift of fellowship so you are not isolated. They are your first human covering. Your family could be one in which you are born into (home), or one in which you grew with (society).

With the progression of years, you were presumably registered in a learning institution, which is also a composition of different families. All these were given to enrich your garden. These also offer a degree of covering or protection to you. It is also a natural gift (security) given to you because you belong to that environment. To sustain these, you have to rely on God.

More so, it is known from times past that some people are born great, because of their lineage, while some acquire greatness, as they proceed with life. It does not matter where you begin, what matters most of all is where you end. Some start small, and go on to become great while others go on to become greater, it is only when people take God out that they experience reversal of fortune.

> It does not matter where you begin, what matters most of all is where you end.

Ecclesiastes 7 vs. 8

Genesis 10 verse 8 tells of a certain man, Nimrod. All that was mentioned of his background was his father's name, Cush. The bible records that this man went ahead and became a mighty one on earth. He was not only mighty before men; he was also mighty before God. It is God's desire that your garden should blossom now and even after you are gone. May God make you like Nimrod in Jesus' name. Amen.

Genesis 10 verse 8

As earlier said, a gift is anything that can improve the quality of life, and it includes some life experiences. Those who are great or have grown to become great are those who have learnt to diligently serve their environment with their gifts (via finance, skills, e.t.c). They put their garden to full use. Biblical examples of those who used their seed to achieve a glorious garden of destiny include:

- **David** — He used his seed (experience with the lion and the bear) to remove the oppressor from Israel. In the end, he had a glorious garden of destiny. **1ˢᵗ Samuel 17 vs. 37**
- **Samuel** — His seed (discipline) helped him judge Israel well. **1st Samuel 7 vs. 15-17**
- **Wiseman** — The wise men blessed Jesus with their (seed) gifts. You know what happens to people who give to God. They never lack. They left their comfort zone to seek a baby in "a stranger's farm". Don't you think God made their gardens more comfortable from then onwards? **Matthew 1 vs. 11**.
- **Esther** — Esther used her gift (attitude and beauty) to influence the King into preserving the Jews from being exterminated. Her reign was characterised by God's glory. **Esther 8 vs. 5-6**
- **Joseph** — He used his seed (gift) service to preserve humanity, when there was famine in Egypt. You see his story challenging us today. **Genesis 45 vs. 5-8**
- **Joshua and Caleb** — Through words of encouragements, they used their (seed) positive reports to encourage Moses, and the people were able to possess their portion of the earth, as the Lord has promised them. **Numbers 13 vs. 30**

Others include:

- Moses used his rod (seed) to deliver Israel from the bondage.
- Samson's strength (seed) delivered Israel from their oppressors.
- Job's prayer of intercession (seed) saved his friends
- Solomon's wisdom (seed) was applied in solving his people's problems
- The sacrifice of Jesus (gift) restored us back to God.

The physical bounds are not that easy to maintain. We have seen the need to have loose soil and break up what is required for growth. We have also seen how this process of breaking up exposes all manner of mess.

However, God intends that you continue from where He stopped in the Garden of Eden; His desire is for you to become His fellow worker (gardener) on earth. You must proceed with the breakage; and ensure that your mind is connected to the spirit of God. Only the mind of Christ, present in the life of an individual can arrest the level of filth that is revealed in some breakages. I thought it was a joke, the night I had a premonition that the devil was determined to get my mind. I can only stand and thank God today that as the devil struck; I was given grace to hold onto the word of God in the years that followed. I would have been put away because of what I was hearing, but I thank God that His word and the prayers of the saints arrested it.

More so, among the great, generational skeletons do exist. The Holy Spirit told me that when He inspires people to unveil their closets (experience), the motive is not to uncover and ridicule people. In fact, in doing so, one would be uncovering oneself. The bible commands us to cover one another's nakedness. Where the motive is wrong, hurts and pains are inevitable. With the right motives, lives are enriched and growth is certain.

The by-product of a wrong motive may result in hatred and curse, which is the last thing you want to be involved with as a Christian. This reminds me of a caption I once read as a child. *"Hatred does you more harm than the person that hurt you. Hatred demeans you"*.

Before the attack on my mind, the devil subtlely cornered me into a place where I was playing *"mini god"* to people. I was trying to make everyone comfortable. This invariably nearly altered my motives from serving God to serving man. The result was horrifying. Everyone around found this displeasing, because their expectations could not be met. Then the accuser of the brethren decided to do some over timework by employing "midnight vultures ". The motive was to stir up hatred in my heart against people; including those that I knew loved me. The Holy Spirit encouraged me from the scriptures:

> **Proverbs 10 vs. 12** *"Hatred stirs up strife, but love covers all sins".*

It is easier to say preach this than experience it. If you ever see the rod of the wicked in your garden, after doing all you need to, you would be bitter. The rod comes to insult your foundation. I had always known that cursing was not Christian like, but after a very long time, it occurred to me that God said that we should cut off anything that attracts death. I had to start cursing the spirits responsible for the arrow. It was not a pleasant experience. I should have felt better, but I just felt empty and devoid of my good virtues. That was when I knew I had to change my strategy. This is what I have been doing prayerfully.

Proverbs 11 vs. 12

Lastly, as I continued to labour in prayer and intentional love, one morning, the Holy Spirit opened my mind to the word of God in Isaiah—an illustration on how to deal with the accuser of brethren.

Isaiah 54 vs. 17

I was led to encourage some of the people that were being accused constantly to pray against the accuser of the brethren. The result, I got was a resounding victory in that area and the devil told me he was leaving with his entourage and never coming back. You cannot imagine how delighted I felt at the outcome.

Expose your closet under the Holy Spirit's guidance. Let God open your eyes to a treasure in your closet. Bless your world with your discovery.

The Spiritual Estate

Mark 4 vs. 20 *"But the good soil represents those who hear and accept God's message and produce a huge harvest-thirty, sixty, or even a hundred times as much as had been planted".*

As you respect your physical boundaries (your relationship with your family, others and God), you must also guard your spiritual estate. Your spiritual estate is the state where you are in constant touch with God alone. This is where your destiny is guaranteed to end up well. One ofw the ways of ensuring this is through His word. God's words are seeds and when spoken, they have the ability to provide comfort to people, ease tensed environments, and give directions when in doubt. With the seed of His word, you can create the right environment for your garden of destiny.

Psalm 119 vs. 130

The spiritual environment can also be an atmosphere of godliness (friendliness, peace, hard work) or ungodliness (coldness, war, laziness e.t.c). All these are influenced by the abstract world; characterised by visions, ideas, and dreams; which may be positive or negative.

One of the experiences known to man is the dream world. This spiritual can influence the ambience of your garden. History has proved that people's lives have been affected positively and negatively by them. Are you gifted, and you have not discovered it. Do you have dreams and discard them because they appear to have no meaning? If so, you need to ask God for clarity. This is because some seeds come through this medium. Fantastic ideas have being produced through surrealism. **Habakkuk 2 vs. 2-3**

Majority of what I am sharing with you has to do with the inspirations God gave me through dreams. Many people do dream but are not able to discern the meaning. While some completely ignore their dreams, others lay so much emphasis on it until it becomes bondage. Do not worry you are not alone. I have been there and back, and I am happy to tell you, as God told me, *"You have all you need"*. Whatever you need, will come from you.

What are dreams? Dreams are windows into men's spirits. They are a reflection of what the sub conscious picks up as men interact with their environment and with one another. They can be positive or negative, and can only be guided by God's expectation. This is why you need the seed of His word to discern the way forward. The spirit of man is subject to manipulation, but the spirit that agrees with the word of God would bless your life ultimately. The Holy Spirit is one in the universe – The Father of Spirits; that testifies that the word of God is one. Remember that you need to live your life the way God expects you, not another man's.

What are dreams? How can they influence our lives, and how can we use them to bless our environment? Let us look closely at the abstract world (dream). Dreams and visions are a window to catching a glimpse of what the spiritual world proposes for you or for someone else. Let us consider biblical examples of those who caught some seeds (ideas) from the dream world and how they used them to enrich their garden of destiny and bless their sphere of influence.

- ➢ For conviction – to encourage people, live a godly lifestyle. A biblical example of this is King Nebuchadnezzar. He tried to be equal with God and got into a mess. **Daniel 4 vs. 33-34**.
- ➢ For exaltation and promotion – to create an atmosphere for possibilities. It was Pharaoh's dream that God used to promote Joseph. **Genesis 41 vs. 39-40**.
- ➢ For warning – it warns people of impending danger. The wise men were warned not to return to Herod, because he secretly nursed the intention of killing Jesus. **Matthew 2 vs. 12**.
- ➢ For guidance – Joseph was guided to and from Nazareth, to protect Jesus from Herod. **Matthew 2 vs. 13**
- ➢ For consolation – It inspires people in the face of hopelessness. Jacob saw a vision of heaven as he was sleeping on a stone. This was while he was running away from his brother, after stealing his blessings. **Genesis 28 vs. 16-17**

➤ For inspiration—God sharpened Abraham's vision and faith by encouraging him to look at the stars. **Genesis 15 vs. 5-6**.

➤ For favour, the king could not sleep at night, because God wanted to favour Mordecaiah. **Esther6 vs. 1-2**

➤ For assurance—God assured Solomon of his support after he had given a thousand burnt offering. **1ˢᵗ kings 3 vs. 10-12**.

> No dream is fixed or bound to happen. The only fixed thing is the word of God.

However, the fact that it happened in the dream world (spiritual environment) does not mean that it would happen in reality. As mentioned earlier, God is a businessperson, which means He is good at negotiating. When there is a proposal in the spirit realm to execute a task, God permits people to see it—at times clearly, and at times in parables. **Genesis 18 vs. 17,** Jeremiah **23 vs. 28** It is for those that He has given this gift (insight) to negotiate with Him. No dream is fixed or bound to happen. The only fixed thing is the word of God.

Psalm 119 vs. 89

Grab your tool for negotiation now. Influence the outcome of your dreams. Live the will of God for you.

The Cultural Aura

Jeremiah 17 vs. 8 *"They are like trees planted along a riverbank, with roots that reach deep into the water. Such trees are not bothered by the heat or worried by long months of drought. Their leaves stay green, and they go right on producing delicious fruit".*

How pleasant would life be, if you are like one of the trees described above? Think about your life and the lives of those around you as described above. Does this not connote paradise? I want you to believe that this is what the Lord wants you to be. This is the kind of environment He intends you be part of. This is what the word, that cannot lie expects of your garden of destiny and its environs.

The cultural aura is where you find yourself developing, beautifying and enriching the lives of others. It is where you find people who share the same way of spiritual life co-habiting together. Cultural ethics starts with you. The way you relate with your person; what you believe to be spiritual and what the bible says concerning these.

How do these influence your circle? Through service. Serving your cultural environment would require the deployment of your gifts. One of the ways of expressing this is though transparent leadership (or followership). This is nothing new, as every successful leader would testify that transparency is one of the most vital keys to effective leadership. This means that you must allow people look into your garden and make their own judgements based on informed decisions. To do this effectively, you may have to rise above certain expectations imposed by the culture in which you find yourself. It is not a call to disorderliness. God should not be viewed as being disorderly. What appears to be disorderly may be a way to bring about progress in any society or culture.

What is culture? Culture and tradition refer to the way of life of people. It varies from one place to the next, depending on where you are on the globe. Who determines the values and system of beliefs guiding people in a given location? It is the people in the area. How do they achieve this? By observing their environment (weather, climate, e.t.c), their people . . . . they then come together, draw up an acceptable programme of beliefs and values that would enrich the lifestyles of their people. As a Christian, your cultural environment includes your primary place of worship. Remember that you are created to be a well-watered garden. Take advantage of the way of life of where you are. No life thrives independent of its cultural context.

So therefore, it can be concluded that culture and tradition is what works for people based on where they are at and what they understand. For example, what is agreeable in the North Pole may not be acceptable in the South Pole. In addition, what is agreeable in one generation may not be acceptable in the next.

This means that you have to understand the cultural environment of your garden, so you can know how it influences your growth. Not every seed can thrive in all cultural environments. When you see a well-watered garden (great achievers), you will find harmony between the environment, the growth processes and product. Endeavour to align your garden with others, that the blessings of God can flow unhindered in your environment.

1st Corinthians 12 vs. 25

More so, the great achievers have found themselves living between two worlds—theirs and others, and have chosen to accept both. Your way of life is good, but may not be acceptable at the other end of the globe. If you would influence people to part with their money, you must be prepared to leave your world, and embrace theirs. I am not suggesting that you ignore or throw your tradition away; there is always a place for it. This is where culture starts. Hold your culture and belief in your weaker hand (you may need to enlighten others as you interact with them), and with the stronger arm, aggressively grab what the other person has to offer. It is not being greedy, it is being smart; after all two hands clap in order to make a joyful noise.

However, before you grab or accept anything from anyone, to enrich your garden, you need to inspect it, get rid of what is not applicable to your garden, hold fast to what you need or what is in line with your destination. The reaction of some cultures to certain abilities makes it difficult for people to get the necessary help that is required. This results in people not realising their full potentials. Thus all who find themselves within that culture hide in their closet and cry silently, hoping that somehow, somewhere, some day, relieve would come. If you find yourself in this situation, do what Israel did when they were in Egypt. Cry out to God.

> **Psalm 22 vs. 5** *"They cried to you, and were delivered; they trusted in you, and were not ashamed"*.

This is not a call to blame the cultures, but to encourage those within them to receive courage, rise above the norm, and reach out for the help they need. That is vital in enriching your garden. There is tremendous blessing in respecting the culture you find yourself. This may not be the culture you were born. A biblical example of someone who although married a famous and wealthy man, and respected the culture she found herself was Ruth. She came into the land with the mindset of accepting the people and their values (culture). In exchange for this, the people blessed her and she became a vehicle through which God was going to bless humanity. This is your reward for embracing the culture of those you interact. **Ruth 1 vs. 16-17**

No matter how well hidden a garden is, as soon as it begins to blossom, it becomes obvious to everyone. Recently the Holy Spirit told me that although we are seeing the manifestations of the sons and daughters of God, certain belief systems is still hindering some. Growth and general development is being hindered because very few people are prepared to rise above certain belief systems and be transparent (pass the baton of experience and knowledge for others to build on). This is due to the anticipated ridicule that they think may follow their actions.

However, I believe that God would allow you go through some not too pleasant experience (seed) in a graceful manner, so that you can pass the baton well. You can give this gift (seed) to others in a similar situation in the culture you find yourself.

Deuteronomy 6 vs. 7

This implies that the strongholds we have built to hide these skeletons in our closets must come down. This should not be born out of pride, but to identify with others (financially, spiritually, emotionally, e.t.c) so they can see what lies ahead.

Then they know that they do not have to struggle alone. Those skeletons can be very nasty when you confront them alone in your closet. They are like thorns and thistles in your garden. Getting rid of them can be tedious and painful, if you are not very careful in your approach.

> This implies that the strongholds we have built to hide the skeletons in our closets must come down.

However, the refusal to answer to the call to expose and deal with your closet could be devastating. Imagine allowing the thorns and thistles to grow and thrive with your plantation. It is more likely that it is the thorns and thistles that will survive. The real trees and flowers would not manifest. They'll be choked. Ask the inhabitants of Sodom and Gomorrah. Everyone in Sodom and Gomorrah was doing her own thing in their closet when the Lord visited them unannounced. Their filthiness stopped them from noticing His presence in their midst. Lot was able to sense it because he was a righteous man. He had taken charge of his spiritual gift (walk with God) in the culture he found himself.

God did not need to visit Sodom and Gomorrah to execute judgement, He could have done it straight away, but in His loving kindness, He chose to visit them first. This was to give them room to repent. God can visit you at any time of the day *(or anytime in your life)*. He visited Abraham at the heat of the day *(a rough season of life)* and He visited Lot at the cool of the day *(a smooth season of life)*. **Genesis 18 vs. 1, Genesis 19 vs. 1**

Perhaps you have invited the enemy into your garden (we all have consciously or sub consciously at one time or the other) or visited him yourself, and you feel that thorns and thistles have crept into your closet. You may even be in God's camp right now, but still carrying a skeleton that you may have inherited. Do not worry, it is not permanent. Remember any time Israel did evil in the sight of God, and they cried out to Him, He heard them. They trusted Him and they were not ashamed.

Answer the call of God today. Let Him show you how to handle your affairs. Let God respond to your tears now.

Overcoming Environmental Challenges

Matthew 13 vs. 38 *"The field is the world, the good seeds are the sons of the kingdom, but the tares are the sons of the wicked one".*

Life is full of struggles and the contender is always attempting to put people out of the will of God, despite God desiring your's desire for their garden to be good. Right from creation when God put man in the Garden of Eden, we see the devil contending with man. In the book of Job, when the sons of God gathered, the devil also joined. The book of Matthew now confirms that as you and I are part of the sons (and daughters) of the kingdom in this world, the sons of the wicked are also among us. The messenger of satan is the spirit that lurks around to wait for those who would deny the word of God and listen to him.

There was a time as I prayed, I hear the contender; struggling for my quiet time with God. A God mocker! They initially sound nice to those who are not spiritually discerned, but they are a deviation from the norm. There are times when I go into a church service, and they want to preach their own sermon against the preacher. God calls them "the accuser of the brethren", accusing them day and night before God. They are principalities and powers that preside over the area. Like earlier said, Isaiah 54 vs. 17 was the final blow that took care of the situation.

This is the reason why we cannot afford to be ignorant. Yes, God wants to enrich our gardens, but we must be mindful of the evil one that lurks around. The only way this would happen is for us to live in harmony with one another and with God. The divine power of God cannot be mocked; it has given us access to all things, including deliverance from elemental spirits.

When the devil badly contended with my mind, I prayed continuously, and I took extra care to embrace the sound words I had acquired in my Christian journey. I went the extra mile to "become a fool for Christ". I knew letting go of the brethren was destructive, so I had to take extra care to relate with the brethren.

Philippians 2 vs. 3

Every garden can thrive well; and most environments have the potential to be good. They can respond to God's call to feed the poor, cover the naked, provide for the needy, e.t.c. This is because the inhabitants are made in God's image and after God's likeness. If people see that you are hungry (spiritual, physical, financial, emotional, and any other form of deprivation), they would act according to how they are led.

However, when people give you food, you need to decide for yourself if you would eat it, and in what quantity. Your decision would be based on the quality — in normal circumstances, you would not eat anything that is not wholesome to your dietary habits. For example, if God has called you to be a medical practioner, and a musician offers you the food of music, because of hunger, accept it gratefully. Eat a little to gain the experience and knowledge, but do not run off to the market to buy a truckload of music products. **Genesis 1 vs. 26-27**

On the other hand, if you are being offered garden products, grab it, eat it, find out more about it, run to the market, buy it, bring it home, read the manual, and use it accordingly.

More so, if the inhabitants of our environment are so generous with their gifts, what are the factors that might inhibit our motivation to bless them in return with our gifts (seed)? One of the first challenges you would encounter in the course of discovering and trying to till your garden and cultivate your seed (gift) within your environment would be people's reluctance to change.

This may initially generate some anger within you, which if not checked, would destroy both your garden and your gift. As earlier discussed in the previous chapter, transparency is another factor that you need to exhibit in a wise way. This is because of the people's attitude to certain abilities. This may mean that you have to relate with them from a distance. At such times, you should remember that transparency is vital in persuading people to accept what you offer. The godly way to do this is to be like Adam and Eve.

Genesis 2 verse 25

Those you communicate with from a distance will respond to you from a distance. The danger here is that anything can happen in between from no communication to poor communication. Well there is really nothing you can do about this. You only have to pray for God to take His rightful place in the scheme of things.

More so, handling your closet will require in a way that will be a blessing to all (you and those you share the closet with) involves being tactful.

More so, in developing your garden, you must do it in a way that it would not constitute a nuisance (encroach into) to your neighbour's garden. This is because our gardens (lives) have a way of influencing our neighbour's.

Most of the Christians that challenged my growth were people who were willing to expose some of the contents in their closet. As I peeped into them, they influenced mine. They overcame, so am I learning to overcome and so would you, in Jesus' name. Amen.

They were not afraid to be naked, and this encouraged me to respond to them. Like Adam and Eve, they were naked, and not ashamed. They dared to deal with some of those skeletons in their closet. As they did this in public, I was encouraged to examine mine. These thorns and thistles sure do hurt to the bones and marrow. The rewards of getting rid of them is refreshing to the soul.

I have been tending to my garden in private, and now having almost perfected the act, by the power of the Holy Spirit, I can now expose it in public. Therefore, as my predecessors have blessed me with their gifts (seeds), so I must bless you with mine from my garden of destiny.

1ˢᵗ Corinthians 3 vs. 7

In conclusion, look to Jesus, the seed giver. Look to God who encourages the growth. Allow yourself the opportunity to have a rich garden.

PART 2:
The Growth And The Harvest

 **Isaiah 27 vs. 3** *"I, the Lord, will watch over it and tend its fruitful vines. Each day I will water them; day and night I will watch to keep enemies away"*.

EXOTIC INCREASE

Psalm 1 vs. 3 *"He shall be like a tree planted by the rivers of water that brings forth its fruit in its season, whose leaf also shall not wither; And whatever he does shall prosper.*

The Introduction

Isaiah 30 vs. 23 *"Then He will give the rain for your seed with which you sow the ground, and bread of the increase of the earth; It will be fat and plentiful. In that day your cattle will feed in large pastures".*

In this part, we would see how God designed, formed and blessed the earth—air above with all in it, waters with marine life and the dry ground with vegetation. We also know that God blessed all these and commanded them to work for his glory. He then made man and put him in the garden to produce qualitative results in immeasurable quantity. Man now has to take advantage of all the resources to make a success of life.

You are God's garden with potentials to blossom, so you can determine your fate. As you walk with Him, you would also see the provisions God made to ensure you blossom well in your garden and how easily assessable these provisions are. Gaining access to God's provision is a challenge to many. Knowledge is the key that opens your garden to provisions, so key into the revelations the Holy Spirit would drop in your mind as you continue reading this book.

More so, what you want is God's approval of "very good". The world can commend you, and you would not amount to much at the end of the day, but if God confirms you, you would amaze yourself. His confirmation puts you in the position where He cannot back off from your garden. Walk with Him and let Jesus show you the path.

The resources you need are available now, right where you are. Your garden can only blossom where you constructively utilise the resources available where you are. They are meant to adapt to the environment, so you need to control the environment. As you do this, you are guaranteed to succeed at the right time and in the right season. You would not be out of time, but in time.

Psalm 1 vs. 3

Also, remember that your garden is not for your benefit only. If you live alone, no matter how beautiful and therapeutic the garden is, you would crave for fellowship (relationship with others) some times. This also requires you controlling the environment, so it can accommodate fellowship.

Take an inventory of the resources at your disposal today. Consider the results in your life and your desired outcome. Use them to achieve and maintain a well-balanced garden.

Divine Aid

Genesis 2 vs. 10 *"A river flowed from the land of Eden, watering the garden and then dividing into four branches".*

A chieving a well balanced garden can only be possible through divine aid. You can see this illustration from the creation of the first garden in Eden. God made the waters, gathered them together and then channelled them to wet the earth. This was a work of the divine head—God the father, Son and Holy Spirit. Divine aid is therefore help that comes from the divine head (divinity). The divine head is also known as the triune God; the three in one God.

In the book of John 1, the bible describes God as the God that existed in the beginning. He initiated the beginning of all you know and would ever be. In Genesis 1, the heavens and earth were created by the power of the spoken word, in the presence of the Spirit of God. The same word we talk about was expressed in the person of Jesus Christ, when He came to live on earth. When He left, the Spirit of God continued to dwell amongst you, and testify to the authenticity and efficacy of the word. Acts 1 vs. 8. As it was in the beginning, so is it today. The spirit is present. Your garden may not have formed yet, it does not matter. The spirit is waiting on you. The spirit waited for God to speak at creation, so He has to wait for you as well.

More so, God would open your inner eyes to the right soil, and as you plant your seed, the other factors that would be required for growth to take place is the rain. This occurs naturally, and is not dependent or controlled by man, but God. It is however possible for man to influence their effect on the earth. Here I choose to characterise the rain and the sun by your prayers and the word (light) of God.

Why is the rain (divine assistance) important? They come to add nutrients (ability) to the crops in order for it to mature (produce). You cannot do much without praying; neither can you achieve anything of eternal value without the word of God. These factors add potential to your seed and make it different to others (unique). **Zechariah 10 vs. 1**

Normally when it rains, it waters the area, so does your garden and the blessings of God. The blessing comes to enrich your garden and its environs. To achieve a wholesome environment, your prayer, which is an aid (gift), must therefore cover your environment. Prayer is therefore the seed that commands divine aid, necessary for the garden to blossom and become therapeutic (peaceful and quiet).

Can you imagine an environment without godly leaders? Every attempt at achieving a beautiful therapeutic garden would fail. Ungodliness and disorderliness would choke the beauty and calm. This is the why you need to pray; for godliness to reign in your environment and leadership. You need it, so does your leaders. **1ˢᵗ Timothy 2 vs. 2**

How ever, there are times when the land may experience drought (because of sin). At such times, there would be little or no rain, and this may invariably affects the growth of your seed. Divine help may be delayed, but with persistence, it would surely come.

> Divine help may be delayed, but with persistence, it would surely come.

The rain (divine help) is necessary for every stage of development of your seed, regardless of the type. As man cannot restrain the rain, so no one can restrain the effect of the prayer and the word of God spoken over your seed, in the presence of the Holy Spirit. **1st Kings 9 vs. 3**

Having met all the conditions; and no evidence of growth, do not give up, but continue in prayer and the word. Elijah did that when there was a drought in Israel and God responded positively. **1ˢᵗ Kings 18 vs. 1-2**

There was a season between the promise and its materialisation. Many prophesises (confirming the word of God) went forth until there was a physical manifestation. **1st Kings 18 vs. 41-45.**

After you have done all you know to do, do not faint, the God that commanded from the beginning and it was so, is still around. His word was, is and is to come. You may not be able to understand how divine aid operates, but it does. **James 5 vs. 7**

You have assurance from God that He would hear you when you call. You can be sure that He would rain His blessings on you, when you seek Him. You can be confident that you would receive divine aid, as you wait on Him.

The Facilitator

Song of Solomon 4 vs. 16 *"Awake, north wind! Come, south wind! Blow on my garden and waft its lovely perfume to my lover. Let him come into his garden and eat its choicest fruits."*

This is a prophetic command, placing a demand for the wind to blow upon a portion of the earth, so its sweet fragrance can be released on the inhabitant. The wind is meant to facilitate the relaxation of the subject in his garden. A facilitator is an aid assigned to speed up a task or a person's achievement.

In parallel, prayer can also be seen as a tool to facilitate our walk with God in order to achieve our desired goal. The wind; a natural air in motion, is a facilitator for the rain. Depending on where you are, as it blows, you may choose to fall asleep. The air in motion however carries lot of things with it and deposits it randomly. The deposit is for anyone who needs it. So therefore, if every time the wind blows, you decide to fall asleep, you may not be a partaker of heaven's fringe benefits. Your sleep therefore must be within reasonable and appropriate time. Make sure that you are awake at the time when the kind of fringe benefit you are looking for is about to be delivered. When is this? No one but God knows. His encouragement to you is to 'watch and pray'. **Proverbs 20 vs. 13**

More so, the Holy Spirit is also a facilitator; characterised as a gushing wind to help you when you pray. My mum was the first to show me a technique she was taught to use when in doubt. Today, when in doubt as to the way forward, or am in search of a missing item, I usually pray and see results. I just say *"Father, your spirit is a candle that searches all things, please help me search for my . . . ."* It always works.

The facilitator, the wind can also, be seen as opportunities life offers to all. One of the things that would begin to happen once you begin to pray is that God would begin to sharpen your vision (open your eyes to see opportunities you did not see previously). Hagar and Ishmael in Genesis are biblical examples of this. They were both dying of thirst, Ishmael wept (prayed) and God opened the eyes of his provider (Hagar) to see the provision (a pool of water). **Genesis 21 vs. 17-19**

Today, I thank God for my life. Unlike few people, I was unsettled for years. I was always planning independently, but always failed to lived up to the plan. Thank God, He intervened and gave me the opportunity to organise myself (*not only my thoughts and stories*). He gave me the opportunity to be me, to understand and appreciate myself and to live in time. It has been almost twenty years of rigorous exercise learning to wait on God. **2nd Corinthians 9 vs. 10**

Opportunity also refers to a chance or a break into something that may be beneficial. Most times, it carries a positive connotation, and occasionally, it may be negative. One just needs to be able to discern between the two. As earlier mentioned, the wind carries many things as it moves and some of them help the flowers grow. The same is true for life's opportunities. There is a time for every thing and there are opportunities every time and everywhere. In addition, opportunities may be physical (promotion, progress, e.t.c), spiritual (favour, grace, mercy). **Ecclesiastes 9 vs. 11**

You can also create positive opportunities for your garden to thrive by setting certain standards to monitor the growth and these include the following:

- ➢ Sowing seeds (money, grace, mercy, forgiveness, service, kindness, and e.t.c) into the lives of others. Remember that you can never out give God; He gave you all you have. **Proverbs 19 vs. 17**
- ➢ Preparing: Having seen the numerous opportunities, you must use them to your advantage. Success is the point you get to where adequate preparation meets with desired opportunity; the level when the required outcome is realised. This means that preparation is an ongoing exercise. Lack of adequate preparation leads to frustration and failure (inability to get the desired result). **Ecclesiastes 11 vs. 4.**
- ➢ Avoiding dead ends (desperate positions): before you prepare for any journey, it is assumed that you have a destination in mind. I remember on my way to church one morning, I was running quite late, and the trains

were terribly delayed so I had to opt for the ferry. To my dismay, the other end of the river was a dead end on that day; there were many diversions on the way, so there was no direct access to our destination. We decided to get out of the dead end, to a bus stop that offered more opportunities.

Failure to get out of the dead end often leads to stagnation, which weakens knowledge and destroys understanding. If you choose to tarry there, after a while, you would be no different from the one who with no knowledge. Encourage mind-stimulating activities to keep you from getting stagnant. **Proverbs 21 vs. 16**.

> There is a time for every thing and there are opportunities every time and everywhere.

> ➤ Avoiding distractions: In life, there would be many distractions, and your ability to remain focused is what makes you succeed. I remember a story I was told, that helps me put my responses in check. The story was told of two men who worked in the same building. Every morning they arrived at the same time, and alighted from the lift.

One gets off at the seventh floor, spit at the one going to the tenth floor, and leaves in disdain. This continued daily until the liftboy made an inquiry on why the man working on the tenth floor made no response. He turned to the liftboy and said, "If I go after him, I would not get to the tenth floor, and if I get there, I would be late". Distraction is what the man working on the seventh floor posed to the other man on the tenth floor. God can and he would deliver you from every form of distraction on the way. **Ezra 8 vs. 31**

➢ Come out of the potholes: The potholes in your life are the damaged spots on your way to your destination, as you journey onwards. No one is exempted from this, as it is a result posed by life's challenges. The way out is to get out of it. Do not get caught in it, resolve to get out. You can do this through prayers and dedication to hard work. **Ecclesiastes 10 vs. 18.**

You have a positive and definite assurance from God that if you would dare to try, every time you fall into the pothole of life, with God, you would get out. **Proverbs 24 vs. 16**

Remember that it is God who commands the wind to release the freshness of the environment on you. The bible calls you the aroma of Christ, and this is what would bring about the favour you need to accelerate and cause you to be in tune with time. A person who gives off a good aroma is attractive to all and attracts favour. God's favour is the favour that would make you receive the empowerment to survive, and it all depends on how good you smell. Pray that the Lord would command the freshness of your environment on you, in Jesus' name. Amen.

In conclusion, remember, the fact that you miss an opportunity does not mean that it is over. I remember the film "The sound of music". Maria's ambition was to be a nun, but she had gifts that could bless the world. The reverend mother sent her out with the following farewell message, which is the same message for you: *"When the Lord closes the door, some where He opens a window".*

Therefore, look out for the window of opportunities around you. Use the opportunities God has given you freely. Escape into the progress already waiting for you.

The Root Of Destiny

Colossians 2 vs. 7 *"Let your roots grow down into him and draw up nourishment from him, so you will grow in faith, strong and vigorous in the truth you were taught. Let your lives overflow with thanksgiving for all he has done".*

The root of a tree is the part that holds or supports it firmly to the ground; the reason for its standing. The root of destiny is therefore the reason or foundation for a glorious (life) garden. It is the basis for your fate. It is the reason you would want to thrive well. It is important; in order to provide a strong base for your garden to thrive well. If your life finds its root in God, you would discover a healthy way of living and strong reasons to live; which would make you praise God.

The period between the planting of the seed and the production of fruit, is the waiting period. Due to several factors, it could also be a time of anxiety. One is certain though, God has promised to look after you. You only need to look forward to the best that He has to offer. **Matthew 6 vs. 34**.

The seed that has been planted develop roots underground (in secret). The indispensability of these roots cannot be disputed. Some roots are useful in themselves e.g. crops and tubers (carrots, cabbages, potatoes, e.t.c), while others offer strength and support to the plants and trees that grow out of the ground. Pockets of endeavour that you put into your life make up your destiny. To do this in a qualitative manner, you need wisdom (adequate and appropriate knowledge). **Proverbs 24 vs. 14.**
It is expected that where the seed has been sown in the soil, with the right conditions, the next thing that happens underground is the development of the root. No one sees or knows this phase, except the person responsible for the planting.

More so, once you have discovered your gift (the seed), and the environmental conditions have been addressed (the soil), the next phase would be to start working it out (from the root). This would be the season when no one is watching, your silent years when it seems that the world is passing you by. It is the season for your root formation and gathering of momentum. This phase is important because your root is the strength for the success of your garden. Good channelling of your roots at these periods would result in outstanding results or fruits that would attract favorable increase. This is one of God's ways of honouring men. **Proverbs 18 vs. 16.**

As discussed in previous chapters, knowing where, when and how to plant the seed for destiny is not enough. You need to obey

His instructions. This would include maximising the resources within your reach and being the best you can be, in any given situation. So how do you maximise the potential of your seed from the root to enrich your destiny?

The illustration God used to explain this title is the "nursing mother principle". A nursing mother is advised to follow the ante natal directives, else she would have to take charge for the outcome of both her child and herself. As you ask God for a glorious destiny, He' ld give it to you in the form of a seed (idea, dream or vision), which is a determinant for your destiny.

However, you can only follow the instructions, if you know what it is. In my early years, while preparing us for an external exam, one my teachers kept on saying to us "the understanding of any question itself is a test". The remark was made when we turned to our friends for clarifications of exam questions during the tests. That was life, but we thank God, we can turn to Him when in doubt.

Jeremiah 33 vs. 3

More so, you need appropriate understanding of the root of your destiny to get your desired result. If you want your dream, ideas or vision to be outstanding, it is godly and wise to inquire from God what the purpose would be. This is how you can use the result to influence your circle of influence and bless your maker. The knowledge would help you take qualitative decisions in the formative years of your aspirations.

Do not forget, this is another pocket of endeavour on your path, to help shape your own destiny as well. Your son cannot be the president of a nation and you would end up a wretch! The only way this would happen is if you abandon him and refuse to relate with his person. Angel Gabriel revealed God's purpose for John the Baptist, to his father. He also gave him the manual and guideline for getting there. **Luke 1 vs. 14-17**

We also know of another man who dared to ask God for the purpose of his child. God not only told him the vision of the child, he gave him a guideline as well. This helped them to tend to the child from the root. **Judges 13 vs. 13-14**.

As a gardener knows the purpose of everything in his garden and tends to it, so does the farmer know the purpose of each seed in his farm, and so does God know the purpose of each seed (dream, vision and idea) in your garden of destiny. To be able to identify with your harvest and be satisfied with the produce, you need to personally tend to it. There is nothing as rewarding in the end, than what you do or are a part.

On the other hand, if you choose to leave it in the hands of others to cultivate, they would nurture the seed (idea, vision, or dream) to the best of their ability, according to the manual they have from God. When this happens, at time of maturity, the person that gets maximum fulfilment is the one who cultivated it, because the person has cultivated it according to the manual he received from God.

To refuse to be part of the development of your seed (idea, vision, or dream) would lead to failure to reap maximum benefit (fulfilment). The grace of God may permit you to taste of the benefit. If you desire pure orange fruits, follow the guidelines for tending to it, else another gardener can carry out a hybrid exercise (and cross your orange seed with another member of the citric family). Although you would see oranges at time of maturity, you do not get a pure orange tree.

In addition, God giving you the manual for seed (idea, vision, or dream) can be compared to a midwife instructing you on how to look after your child. The mid wife is the mid wife, and you are the mother or visionary. If you decide to deviate from the instruction given by the mid wife, based on your age, culture, or ideals, be ready to take charge for the outcome.

However, one may argue *"how about those who for some genuine reasons are not able to tend to their dreams or visions (from the root)?* As you pray and follow, God would lead you to the right people (the Joshuas, Aarons, and Hurs) who would strengthen your hand, not those who would weaken it. There are people that positioned in strategic points in your life that grow with you. **Psalm 18 vs. 33-34**.

God would not give you a seed (dream or vision) that He has not graced you with the ability to handle (directly or indirectly – through people).

Psalm 68 vs. 19

There are times when as a result of prolonged wait, hope is deferred. This is the time you are tempted to take your eyes off God and this is the time the devil would attempt to defraud you. He can only attempt, he

> You can ask God; the source (water) of life to revive your seed (dreams, or vision).

cannot succeed. The bible says that he is 'like a lion', he is not a lion. He is only an imitation, and when the 'real' turns up, it overshadows the imitation. Jesus is the lion (of the tribe of Judah). Jesus is the king of the jungle.

However, if you have not tended to your seed (dream or vision), the way God intends and it has become alien to you, there is hope. Even if it is almost dead, you can thank God; at least it is alive. **Job 14 vs. 7-9**.

You can ask God; the source (water) of life to revive your seed (dreams, or vision). **Jeremiah 15 vs. 19-21**

The key to a strong root is Jesus Christ. The corrective measure to a faulty output is Jesus. The benefit of a well watered garden is Jesus. **Colossians 2 vs. 7**

Be grounded. Remain rooted. Reach for the heights.

The Shoot For Destiny

Isaiah 27 vs. 6 *"In days to come, Jacob shall take root, Israel shall blossom and put forth shoots, and fill the whole world with fruit".*

The shoot of a tree is the part that buds above the ground. Under God's guidance, the seed or gift you nurture in secret (from the root), would blossom and become obvious to the public. Nurturing is an assiduous process. Before you would nurture anything to excellence, you must be well established; that is have a sound understanding of how it functions and what it takes to function.

One of the reasons why God would allow your garden to blossom is for you to be blessed and be a blessing. Others should be able to benefit from your garden as well. That is the way God made the trees of the garden. They were made to be useful to both man and animals. Mark 4 vs. 32. You would need to protect your garden from thorns and thistles (scoffers and mockers) as these do not look nice in the garden.

In like manner, when you go amiss, which we all do from time to time, do not look down on your self. The fact that your approach to one idea messed up does not mean that you should give up on it. This is true; especially when you are convinced; it was God's idea. Remember the story of the prodigal son in Luke 15.

The prodigal son in the bible is an example of a seed raised by his father. This particular son had a different idea (he took the turn for the worse). He wanted to launch out before reaching the age of maturity (immaturity was responsible for the riotous living). **Luke 15 vs. 13**. 'He ended up messing himself up and squandering the family's wealth'.

Like wise, every farmer (visionary) prays that his seed (dream or vision) mature and prospers (outlive them). An understanding of the times is necessary for this to happen. The visionary needs to be in tune with the times with regards to his dreams, knowing what to do and when.

Luke 21 vs. 30

More so, a vision that would endure is one that would understand timing. The prodigal son failed to understand the timing of his vision. Bad timing is one of the biggest causes of death in seed. It leads to failures of dreams and visions. Good timing is a key tool in successful business endeavour. The boy also had the wrong approach (badly applied vision). He did not wait to be given, he demanded for it. A wrong approach to a vision or execution of an idea can kill it. **Luke 15 vs. 12**

However, the bible says that he came to himself (a misdirected vision can be recaptured). He remembered who he was, and decided to defend his right. Until you begin to think right, you cannot move your ideas forward, even if they are divine. The Holy Spirit will not force you to think; He will only inspire and drop ideas in your mind. **Luke 15 vs. 17-19**

The prodigal son knew that as a child of his father, by right, he was entitled to a measure of his father's wealth. This knowledge made him approach his father with confidence, before and after he messed up. On the two occasions, he got what he wanted. You can recapture a misdirected vision by praying. Everything has ears, and everything responds to God's word.

In addition, I can remember the several challenges I faced before this book became a reality. It looked as though the spirit of contention wanted to change the message to what did not make sense, so that I can give up on it. He almost succeeded, but thank God, He could not. Many prayers went into it, coupled with fasting. At a point in time, I began to ask for His presence, character and image in all I think, do and say. That was when my circumstances began to align themselves with the glory of God in my life. **Hosea 2 vs. 21-22**

Whenever you mess up a God given idea, you can always go back to Him and watch as He fixes the errors with joy. God knows the devil more than we do, that is why His area of speciality is making right what the devil mean for evil. Trust Him in all you undertake. **Luke 15 vs. 20**.

> Whenever you mess up a God given idea, you can always go back to Him and watch as He fixes the errors with joy.

In summary, your life cannot experience significant growth,

unless it receives divine aid from above. Any garden that remains connected to water bodies (God's divine provision), would inevitably succeed in their time. A disconnection may lead to loss in time, but as a reconnection is made, there is a recovery and redemption of time, where years lost can be made compensated. **Psalm 1 verse 3**.

Be the fruit bearer in your garden. Be the tree that always rises above the ground. Rise above the challenge posed to your shoot.

The Fruit Of Destiny

Leviticus 26 vs. 4 *"I will send the seasonal rains. The land will then yield its crops, and the trees will produce their fruit"*.

A fruit is one of the products from a tree or the outcome of an endeavour. A tree does not always bear fruit; they are also used for beauty and shade. Any tree that is not seen to be useful is most times cut off.

Under the right condition, the seed you plant would eventually produce fruits (desired results). Anyone can prosper where they are. God is able to show you how, where, what to and what not to do, to prosper. He is also able to show you how to relax and enjoy your progress. He can also give you the blue print for prosperity, at the right time. **Isaiah 48 vs. 17.**

The fruit of your destiny is the product from your garden as it strives to attain a glorious end. Now this outcome can be good, bad, sour or bitter, depending on how the growth process was managed. The planting of the Lord is always good, and most times, He uses man to carry out the processes. Man is left with a choice on how to handle the processes.

In Eden, all the trees were well planted, and there was one that was the tree of decision. On it God allowed the fruit of choice to grow. Man was given the opportunity to trust God solely. Man decided to contend with his freedom and today, every single one of us have to contend with the choices before us and be responsible for the decisions we make. **Genesis 2 vs. 9**

You are God's planting; His seed, and if you let Him guide your growth, you would produce good fruit. In the same vein, if you sow the right seed, and nurture it well, under the guidance of God, it would profit you. It is a gift to enjoy the planting process. **Ecclesiastes 5 vs. 19**.

Most of the time, the fruits would be good and wholesome but there are those occasions when you observe a defect (because of pests and weeds). While pests serve as devourers (destroying what they did not plant), weeds grow with your plants to compete with them for their resources and ultimately destroy them. They grow because someone consciously or sub-consciously drops their seeds on your soil, or because of the wind carrying seeds from other places onto your soil. One thing is sure, you never plant weeds!

What are the defects (pests and weeds) that can mar your desired outcome (the development of your fruit)? They include folly, deceptions, carelessness, pride, and the other works of the flesh. A biblical illustration of this can be found in the story of Samson in Judges 13. He was a gifted man (covenant carrier). The sign of his covenant was the hair on his head and his abstinence from strong drinks (alcohol). They were both physical (accessible to the public), he failed to protect them. **Judges 13: 4-5**.

The Lord planted Samson for a purpose in Israel. The Lords of the Philistines were also from God, but had derailed. That is why they began "acting as weeds" in Samson's life (garden). They observed his fruitfulness and ventured to find out the source of his strength. They wanted to do this, not because they were interested in the God he served, but so they can destroy his gift and continue with business as usual (destroying God's fruits).

Although God planted Samuel, he did not align his life with the word of God, and the consequence was that his garden brought forth a sour fruit named folly. Perhaps Samson was a man given to folly, doing everything that he was not meant to do, e.g. touching dead bodies, drinking wine, relating with strange women, pride (misusing the power of God) e.t.c. The enemy sensed it, and decided to capitalise on it, competing for his life.

Once the Lords of the philistine (weeds) noticed this, they formed an alliance with a flirtatious spirit — spirit of Delilah (the pests). They then employed her to keep him company (scheming and manipulating situations in order to find out what he stood on and what made him thick and different to them). As a christian, you need to be aware of these twin evils (the spirit of Delilah and the Lords of the philistines). They encapsulate the work of the flesh, the lust of the eyes and the pride of life. Their prominence in the world makes them dangerous contenders.

More so, Samson's folly can be compared to the story of a rich man and the thief who visited him. The manipulating thief dined with the rich man and demanded for his money. The rich man brought out his safe and gave the thief a wrong combination for unlocking the safe. The thief kept on trying the different combinations given by the rich man. The rich man thought it was a game, to wine, dine, and mess about with his treasure. The thief knowing what he was after, continued to entertain the rich man's folly, until he could no longer discern between right and wrong.

The rich man ended up giving the right combination to the thief, who opened the safe, took away all the rich man's treasure and left him for dead. His vision and destiny became altered. He could not use his money for a purposeful venture, because he did not have any left. **Ecclesiastes 7 vs. 12**

In Samson's folly, he revealed his source of strength to them. Once they were able to access it (physically), they began to work against him. In the same vein, if what makes you thick is other than God — money, fame, influence, power, e.t.c), it would be easily assessable to the enemy.

Identity crisis is another defect (weed) that can mar your desired outcome (fruit). Perhaps if Samson was conscious of who he was in God, he would not have needed to prove himself and his strength to the Philistines or Delilah. To him, it was a sport or a game, to the Philistine, it was a trap to destroy him and to God, it was plain folly.

Any time a man forgets who he is in God, the devil will have a filled day. He tried it with Eve in the garden and succeeded. He also tried it with the Israelites and succeeded. Thank God that when He tried it with Jesus, he failed, because Jesus knew who He was in God. How about you, do you know who you are in God?

More so, as you interact with the public, you need to ask the Holy Spirit to help you discern the fruits you come in contact with daily. As earlier explained a flirtatious and manipulative spirit is one that comes to wine and dine with a man, with the purpose of destroying him. It is a by-product or the fruit from the tree of deceptiom and lust.

In addition, if a man's boast is in chariots and horses (wealth or tangible things), he becomes an easy prey to the enemy. The enemy can then come in, capture him (bind), mock him (and His God), and destroy his vision. You need to behave well and hold onto the spirit of revelation.

Proverbs 29 vs. 18

The key to Samson's gift (strength) was physical, and he failed to guard it, so it was easy for the enemy to discover and attack. The key to your gift can be guarded from the enemy by placing it in the unshakable and stable hands of God. Stand on the integrity of His word, and like the songwriter, Edward Mote (1834), you too can testify:

> "... On Christ the solid rock I stand, all other ground is sinking sand ....".

Where Jesus is the solid rock on which you stand, then your contender would be contending with Jesus. The consequence of this is that the spirit of the contender would either be changed (saved) or destroyed.

More so, your spirit man will not be easily assessable, unless you expose him (through pride or lust). Thank God today your strength is not in the physical. The bible says that your gift (seed) is hidden in you.

2nd Corinthians 4 vs. 7

God is a covenant maker, not a covenant breaker. No generation can prove Him unfaithful. **Numbers 23 vs. 19.** The covenant of God with Samson was rekindled as his hair grew. As a child of covenant, even when you turn back to God (as the defect grows), the covenant (God's promise to prosper you) will keep speaking and encouraging you to come back. As the hair on Samson's head began to grow, he remembered the covenant God made with Him.

In addition, Samson knew that he can call on God and God would answer. He called and God did not disappoint him. His captors knew the secret of his strength, but forgot that God is not a covenant breaker. They were able to take his vision, but they could not destroy his covenant. Today, no matter how far gone you are from your fruitfulness, you can still call on God and what he did for Samson and the children of Israel, He can do for you. What he did for our fathers He can do for you. **Psalm 22vs 4-5**.

> Even so, God is a covenant maker, not a covenant breaker.

All you need to do to partake and enjoy a lovely fruit from your garden of destiny is to be in right standing with God.

Isaiah 3 vs. 10

Arise to your garden today and tend to its growth now. Watch the Lord of increase prosper your garden. Notice how much fulfilment you get.

Weeding For Destiny

Proverbs 24 vs. 31 *"I saw that it was overgrown with thorns. It was covered with weeds, and its walls were broken down.*

As earlier described, weeds refer to anything that grows with your plants, other than what you planted. They deny your plants of the maximum nutrients they deserve because they grow and compete with them. Hence they must be uprooted.

In the course of your seed developing, you would come across growth inhibitors or weeds. The weeds may look very healthy and good, but they are not your desired outcome, so you have to get rid of them. They may come in all manners and circumstances. Weeds and inhibitors affect your garden and attempt to stunt its growth. No one is a weed or a inhibitor; however, there are certain spirits that operate through people, that produce the same results as weeds and inhibitors in the lives of others. The spirit is a contender that robs the person of life in God. It can even kill.

Matthew 13 vs. 25

The fact that a person is successful does not mean you can hang out with him or her. You would know how much of your resources to invest in a person, once you discover their vision (dreams, and ideas) and values. You are to relate with everyone, but you have to discern whom God wants you to invest more of your time with. There are associations that do not add value to your life, but produce things you do not really need in your life (weeds). You need to be able to discern them, and look for the kind that would produce the desired results in your life.

In the days of Noah, before the flood, it had never rained, so the concept of flood was unimaginable. God gave Noah the vision of building the Ark, which would eventually save his household. Noah relayed his vision publicly and mockery (another weed) was the response that followed. This was because his vision was out of this world, it had never happened before and his neighbours could not take it! **Genesis 2 vs. 5**.

This is true of every seed (divine idea) that God gives to man. Every idea of greatness will initially be mocked. Many people have thrown away their seed (dreams and visions) because they were mocked. Few when told that they would never get to their destinations; heard it but refused to believe it. Their choice to take a positive stand on their dreams led them to achieving their goals-desired outcome. Embrace your dream, and focus on it. As there is a price to pay for every relationship, also there would be a price to pay for a dream or vision that would be accomplished.

More over, you cannot blame the mockers (factors responsible for the weeds), because they were not there when God gave you the seed (idea). You throw your seed (dream) away at your peril! Noah and Lot worked out the vision God gave them, despite the mockers, how about you?

More so as a visionary, you should embrace the fact that people will contend with what they do not understand. You cannot make every body understand. Some would, and some will not. Some would now, and some would later. This is why you should pray to God to wing your speech with "power", so the receiver can hear, and respond to Him, and be influenced as you speak. This is very true, especially when your loved ones (and those in your circle of influence) are involved. Life has more meaning when you are able to share your victories with loved ones. There is no joy being delivered, and finding no loved one to celebrate the moments with. Noah's entire household was saved because of God empowering His word in their hearts.

More so, whoever you are and wherever you find yourself, make sure you are connected to the right people (godly people); they may save your neck! Noah's company was saved because of his right standing with God. Walking with God is not always easy, but it is worth it in the end. Getting rid of the weeds (growth inhibitors) may involve you separating yourself unto God for a while. Once the weeds are out, the tree will produce

> Life has more meaning when you are able to share your victories with loved ones.

wholesome and healthier fruits. This would invariably attract the people God wants you to feed. **Ezekiel 47 vs. 12**.
Remember, the wrong company (weeds) would suffocate anyone who permits them.

Guard your walk with God. Guard your heart. Guard the company you keep.

Prunning For Destiny

> **John 15 vs. 2** *"Every branch in me that does not bear fruit He takes away; and every branch that bears fruit He prunes, that it may bear more fruit".*

In the previous chapter, we saw that it is God's intention that we bear useful fruits. For this to manifest, the leaves of the branches of your tree may require pruning from time to time, so that it can be more productive. This is what pruning is all about. Like weeds, parts of the branches of the tree is cut, so it can grow (perform) better. Success is when you reach the target you set out to achieve. **John 15 vs. 3**.

However, you may have harnessed your gift (planted the right seed, in good faith), but the outcome is not exactly as you planned it. This is when the outcome is below your expectation. It is not the time to be disheartened or give up, but pruning time. Remember that the right seed sown will reach maturity someday and bring forth a harvest, if you refuse to allow discouragement get in the way, as you tend to it. **Proverbs 24 vs. 10.**

More so, an unproductive branch can be compared to anything or person whose level of productivity is way below his capability. It could be a lazy spirit operating in a person or environment. Some environmental factors, such as sickness, disasters, neglect, e.t.c could also be responsible for lack of ability or desire to be productive (laziness). The truth is that no one is born lazy. All human beings are born equal, but nature and nurture is a determinant factor of how each would turn out. Since God is the creator of all and knows all, we would look at what he has to say about this. Let us consider the following scriptures from the bible.

> ONE: **Psalm 24 vs. 1** *"The earth is the Lord's, and all its fullness, the world and those who dwell therein".*
>
> TWO: **Psalm 127 vs. 3** *"Children are a gift from the Lord and the fruit of the womb is His reward".*
>
> THREE: **James 1 vs. 17** *"Every good gift and every perfect gift is from above, and comes down from the Father of lights, with whom there is no variation or shadow of turning".*

Based on these three premises, one can logically conclude on the following:
Adults and children that make up the society (environment), are from God, are good, and perfect gifts, designed to bless

one another. They have been empowered from above to help improve the quality of their gardens. If this is true, why are some environments (branches) easier to live in (more productive) than others? Could the spirit of laziness be responsible? If you notice that your environment (branch) is not as productive because of laziness, take heart. The symptoms are what you see, but the cause is deeper than it looks.

For you to be successful in pruning (solution), you need to examine the cause of the poor productivity (laziness). On doing this, you may be able to control, and minimise it, even if you cannot eradicate it completely. So therefore, we would look at laziness, its nature or root cause and how you can control it.

More so, there are two types of laziness, the first is the type that knows what to do but would not do it. This is the type produced by environmental challenges. The cure to this is motivation and the method is enquiry (finding out the key motivation and applying it). The key motivation must be in alignment with the will of God for you both. The will of God is found in His word. It is the seed of the word of God that would produce God's kind of result. The result you get outside the will of God is perversion — unrealistically domineering and self gratifying.

The second type of laziness is the type that discourages people from thinking well. The cause of this is complex, when you forget who you are in God, and take on the personality of someone else in a higher or lower position. This spirit waits for others to do things, and then imitates them, word for word, act for act, without applying any thinking of their own to the work.

Consequently, they do not develop well, because they do not take time to study what they copy, to see how to improve them. Where this is prevalent in any society, such environment would always lag behind the ones who think well. The ones that progress think well, while the others wait, copy and apply (partially).

Howbeit, some would argue that there are no new wheels, or *"there is nothing new under the earth"*. While this may be true, the down side to those who copy and do not think well is that they often copy every thing, including the mistakes as well. While those who think learn from their lessons and correct them in future endeavours, those who refuse to think well refuse to apply their mental resources to rectify the faults.

In addition to this, you would discover that a lazy environment would produce oppressed citizens. If you think that a lazy spirit prevails in your environment, take charge. Begin to prune out the factors responsible. One of the ways you can start is by praying. There is still hope for you. God has not forgotten you yet. Sin sown as a seed, opens the door to unproductive branches, and it is an anomaly that must be corrected or checked. The bible says **2nd Chronicles 7 vs. 14**.

God always responds to maladies with healing. Most times, the only work required of the person under the influence of this spirit is prayer. God can then release grace and power to work, coupled with work opportunities. From time in memorial, He has been known to operate through missionaries—individuals (like Joseph) or groups. **Psalm 105 vs. 17-19**.

If you are going through a pruning process, where God is fine-tuning the branches of your garden (life), take heart. If it is God, it is for your good and growth. He may not reveal everything to you or to those around you, to avoid distractions. Once He is done, you can then become a 'baton of purpose' ideal for the master's good. At times, not knowing the purpose behind some pruning processes, may lead to betrayer (from you or others). **Genesis 39 vs. 2-3**.

Once the pruning is done, growth is inevitable. The result of a pruned and productive branch is gratitude and repentance (with a determination to go on producing). A productive person is a missionary in his endeavour and should be quick to forgive and help revive others. A lazy environment can be reclaimed and revived. From bible times until now, taking the land has always been a joint effort, not one man's effort. History has it that the missionaries of old operated this way (jointly), and were able to achieve outstanding results. It can be deduced from above that the effect of a defective proceed is unproductivety, laziness is the cause and godly pruning is the corrective measure.

Pruning for destiny is therefore curtailing aspects (branches) of your life (garden) so it would blossom well.

> Once pruning is done, growth is inevitable.

Look into aspects of your life that is underperforming. Prune out the unnecessary bits. Watch your garden blossom again.

Go Spy The Land. Bring Back The Fruits

18

Songs of Solomon 6 vs. 11 *"I went down into the garden of nuts to see the fruits of the valley and to see whether the vine flourished, and the pomegranates budded".*

A garden that has produced well, can afford to become a blessing to others. The gardener can always go out and look for ways in which he can accomplish this, having being through the whole process from seed to production of fruits. The same principle applies to the school system at tertiary level. When one acquires a degree of knowledge, it is expected of him to go out and work. For most schools, they have programmes that encourage their students to go and gain some experience in the office environment. The purpose of this exercise is to help develop and give them a feel of what lies ahead when they eventually leave school.

This is also similar to conducting a market research before launching your product (fruits in the market place). The process include finding out what the demand is in a given area, what alternatives are available to people, how well these alternatives are and how you can rise up to the challenges faced by these alternatives. **Numbers 13 vs. 1-2.**

Moses instructed the children of Israel to go and spy out the land and bring back the fruits. God had given them the land, but He wanted them to have a feel of the land before going in to possess it. Having a feel will help them prepare mentally, physically, emotionally, e.t.c. For you spying out the land may mean exploring the outcome of your seed or ideas. What are the ideas that cross your mind that seem to be outrageous? What are the ideas that cross your mind that seem to be uncommon? What are the ideas that come to mind that seem to be unattainable, yet you get the feeling that you can achieve it if you try?

If God is the one that is leading you, if God is the one that is your source, If God is the one that has the final say in your life, then it's time to launch out of the dream world. Transform your dream into reality. Begin to experiment your ideas.

However, some would say, *"I do not have any ideas with which to launch out"*! Having received the mandate to launch out, how do you launch out? As earlier mentioned, the brain is stimulated through learning. Think over what you have learnt (verbal and written), find out what others have said about it, and finally pray to God to inspire you with fresh ideas.

A while back, I remember praying to God and asking Him to give me an idea that would influence my generation and the ones to come. He is constantly answering that prayer. I am not waiting to see a large manifestation; I can already see Him moving in my spirit. There would be a physical performance of that which He has said.

More so, once you have acquired your desired skills, and wish to develop on it, you would most likely gravitate to where this need can be met. For many people however, once this need has been met, they forget their original purpose and drift off to something else. This explains the reason why some people never see the manifestation of certain projects that they embark on. They quit just before the result shows up. So how do you launch out?

Begin to experiment your ideas. Look for people! Who? Look for those trying to find their way, and be their eye. Look for those who have begun the journey to their destiny and be a blessing to them. Look for those who have achieved something similar, and help them achieve more. It is while you are busy doing this that God would help you launch out. Hebrews 6 vs. 10.

Bear this in mind, as you lend your eyes for others, God will inspire people to lend theirs to you. As you proceed with your vision, God would send people to support you. As you are in your vision, God would inspire men to strengthen you. It may not be those whom you have helped. Let God determine who would be your eye, support, and strength. God's choice would lead to excellence! For many people however, the fear of other people *"stealing"* their vision, and turning it into theirs, keeps them from reaching out to others. I dare to say that God is faithful and as mentioned in Psalm 121 vs. 5 *"The Lord is your keeper; the Lord is your shade at your right hand"*.

One of the privileges of walking with God is that He will guard your property and inform you of the intention of the enemy before he carries it out. This is not calling people your enemies; the devil only inspires them to do the things they do. In other words, pray for them and move on. Another reason why you should not be afraid of people 'stealing your idea' is that their products help improve yours, a forerunner of what you desire to achieve in God. Relax, reach out, and help others.

> Do what He asked you to, and watch the kind of result He will bring your way.

More so, Israel was required to pass through other people's land, but not dispossess it. God forbade Israel (His chosen) to dispossess Lot and Esau's portion. No one can take what is yours and achieve the same result as you would. God is too principled to allow that to happen. This is especially true when you are in His will, doing what He asked you. Whatever they take was what the Lord wanted to use to bless them or their circle. God always replenishes that, which is taken away, to make way for what you really need.

Today, if you are not doing, what God has called you to do because you think some one has stolen your idea, get up, and obey God. Do what He asked you to, and watch the kind of result He will bring your way. More so remember this "there is no new wheel; result is the name of the game. No two-finger prints or ladybirds are alike; the purpose of God for your life cannot be duplicated. Deuteronomy 2 vs. 4-5, 9, 19.

This implies that God would not permit another person wreck your garden, as you stay close to him, while "spying the land".

God is principled in His dealing with all men. Even when you feel wrecked or worthless in your pursuits at blessing others, there is usually an opening (of courage and encouragement) from God to strengthen you.

So therefore, go ahead and spy out the land. Do not forget to bring back the fruits. Brave up and begin to chart your next line of action.

Reproduce And Replenish

Genesis 1 vs. 28 *"And God blessed them and said to them, "Be fruitful and multiply, and fill the earth and subdue it, and have dominion over the fish of the sea, and over the birds of the air, and over every living thing that moves upon the earth".*

Guarded with the results from your research, you can go ahead and reproduce the fruit from your garden for the required purpose. Reproduction refers to the art of replicating a thing, animal or a person. At creation, after God made the earth, the animals (of air sea and land), and man, He blessed each. He gave them all they needed, including the ability to dominate the challenges associated with growth.

He then commanded them to reproduce. It was not an alternative, it was a command, to fail to do this is sin, may incurs the wrath of God. A fruitful person always attracts blessings. Likewise, a fruitful garden is a delight to work in; the gardener is encouraged to remain faithful to the course.

Matthew 25 vs. 23. We have seen how God expects your product to outlive you. For this to apply to your garden there has to be some sort of maintenance culture. God's design for a productive garden is that the crops never fail. Once you have tilled the garden, there should be continuous increase. Leviticus 25 vs. 22.

For this continuity to be sustained there ought to be similarity between the result and its source. This similarity is what binds the two together. For example, some people say that science and God do not mix, but that statement is not true. God laid the principle for life, and every other thing followed. Living things were designed to reproduce after their kind. The purpose of reproduction is to replenish a thing and preserve its existence to avoid extinction. Your garden must therefore replenish itself at every cycle, so that its productivity can be preserved. In the course of doing this, God may open your eye to discover things you never knew.

More over, before a new discovery can be embraced in reality, several tests and hypothesis must have been put forward. Once a new discovery has been made, the person who discovered it is asked to reproduce it in front of other experienced specialists. This is regardless of the person, his origin, or his position in life. It is only when he can do this, that the visionary's theory is accepted and relayed to the public as a fact. Many theories would then be developed based on it, most of which we are all beneficiaries today. You can be numbered as one of the great discoverers if you do it God's way.

There is no seed that that can not be reproduced. If it is a seed (gift), it can be reproduced. For most of people, the problem is not that they do not have any seed (gift); the challenge is reproducing it; to command the desired result (profitability).

God gave man the power of reproduction, in fact, he was created to reproduce and maintain the work of God. To prove that God is a reproductive one, He made Adam, in His image and sent him forth to go and reproduce. To encourage him, He then reproduced Eve. In their presence, He used them to bring forth Cain and Abel. This summed up the first family. This was the first sign of human reproduction that they witnessed. Genesis 1 vs. 28.

More so, God demonstrates the reproduction principle in the redemption of humanity. When He brought you out of the world (sin), He brings you into His kingdom, and then sends you out to go and bring others in (reproduce). Matthew 28 vs. 18-20. God commanded man to reproduce and anything short of this would be rebellion. God would not take back the gift of an unproductive man, because His gifts are irrevocable. However, as in the case of a seed, any seed (gift) not nurtured would invariably die off.

Romans 11 vs. 29

As your garden becomes more fruitful, more opportunities would open for increase of both the fruits and garden expansion. Matthew 25 vs. 29. Reproduction is a mandate for every one and there are principles that govern reproduction. The first is this; if you want a thing to reproduce after its kind, then you must combine it with its like. Once this rule is breached, then what you get is a hybrid of some sort. The second is this; the condition of the environment must be right. This can occur either naturally or in a controlled zone. An example of this is the plant reproduction. Some plants and flowers would only grow in tropical regions. If you desire to grow tropical plants or trees in temperate regions, you would need to create the environment for its growth.

Another principle of reproduction is this; there must be congruency; i.e the parties involved must be willing to reproduce. This is an act of the mind and where this is lacking, there can be no reproduction. Any time the people's will are violated, the result is always frustration and stagnation.

> There is no gift that that cannot be reproduced.

The command to reproduce has been issued; the choice to reproduce is yours and the power to reproduce lies within you. Rise up and do something.

Evaluate And Validate Your Product

Ecclesiastes 2 vs. 9 *"So I became greater than any of the kings who ruled in Jerusalem before me. And with it all, I remained clear-eyed so that I could evaluate all these things".*

Having completed your research and translated the outcome into actions, the next phase is to evaluate your service. You may be productive, but how well would people accept your service in the market place? Do not let the initial success you have be cloud the reality of the situation on ground. Good evaluation of the current situation is necessary.

This would inform your market and either persuade or dissuade them from accepting what you have to offer. The ability to evaluate things comes from God and it is a gift to aid your seed. To evaluate is to consider and pass the right judgement on a matter. Everyone who desires to succeed must have the right perception of his situations.

There are times when you would be required to make a joint evaluation of a matter and there would be times when you would be required to take the decisions alone. It all depends on the present demand. The Spirit of God is one. He was present from the beginning of creation, and He cannot lie. The lie He could not tell from the beginning, He cannot tell now. The same spirit permitted billions of men all over the globe to accept one bible from one generation to another. The same spirit is available to either confirm or reject your judgement, according to the word of God, when it is presented to others.

> **1st Corinthians 14 vs. 29** *"Let two or three prophesy, and let the others evaluate what is said".*

Although in the world, the value you place on your service is negotiable, in the kingdom of God, this may not be the case, especially when it comes to His expectations of you. Some divine transactions may not be possible, if certain conditions are not met. I remember the first time the manuscript of this book was released to the public in 2006. The attacks were cumbersome. I was going to put it away, without going through with the publisher.

I believed that it would be sufficient and I could move to the next one. The testimonies had been shared. Perhaps God wanted me to put a seal on it, to confirm its integrity. The moment I took my eyes off, things began to slow down for me. When I decided to go through with it, God began to work for me again. This was how I knew that God was overseeing the storms of my life, and I was going to come out of it strong.

Romans 8 vs. 18

However, there are times when having fulfilled all the conditions, no one seems to patronise your service. This is the time to be on guard. Let us look at someone who having obeyed God, had to guard his product and service until He got his desired outcome. **Genesis 26 vs. 2-3**.

Isaac had worked hard and was about to obtain his result in the land, when his rivals dispossessed him. This pattern continued and became a cycle. At some point, His natural reaction would have been anger, but he must have considered the value of his service – expected outcome and declined the invitation to get angry.

This is because anger is one of the factors that can devalue your service (especially to your customers). Do not be caught on Anger Avenue, stay off! It devalues your service. From the discovery of your seed (gift) to the production of fruits, you would be doing a lot of movement with your feet. One of the functions of your feet is for stepping, and you would be doing a lot of stepping – *on both grounds and toes*. This is because of the different people you would be encountering in life.

However, the good news is that you are not the only one in the stepping game, every other human being is involved in it as well, and they would be stepping on your toes. This would invariably produce anger occasionally. The value you place on your seed (gift) will invariably affect your response. This is quite difficult because of our human nature. We all want to defend our right. No one wants to be taken for granted.

Also remember that poor anger management is a character deficiency. Whenever a leader's character goes out of the window, those around him are left to bear the consequences. Noah got drunk and exposed himself unknowingly, the aftermath led to him cursing his own sons. This was a boomerang. Genesis 9 verse 20-25.

More so, if you are a parent, your immediate circle of influence would be your family. No matter what your children do to you, do not curse them. Parents who curse their children do so to their own detriment and peril. Bless your children. A man who refuses to bless his children would die in isolation or in the midst of strangers. Be a blessing to other people's children as well. You never lose out when you are a blessing.

A man, who curses his child so that the child becomes a wretch, will find a wretch looking after him in his old age. As a leader, this principle applies as well. There is no gain in cursing your followers; else, you would find your company being run by cursed people. No one would want to bless God there. No use to you. Sometimes I default in this area, and afterwards I go to God and confess to Him. I say 'every thing can be broken, except the word of God, God as the power of the cross breaks all spells and curses' break them all in Jesus' name. Amen. Encourage an atmosphere that blesses God! That is where the spirit of unity thrives and that is where God would command His blessings. Even when people offend you, there is a way out. Give them your gift of forgiveness (service). Remember, it is the influence of negative spirit that moves through whoever is willing to allow them. Forgiveness does not mean keeping people that should leave your life. There are times when forgiveness is just letting go of certain people who are prone to accepting "certain spirit". You need to forgive them and you need to forgive yourself.

You have a gift you can offer to the world. It is called the gift of forgiveness. We all need to give and receive this gift. You do not have to become miserable by refusing to accept the gift, and you do not have to be mean and antagonistic by refusing to give that gift. It is a very cheap gift to give the world. In return for your service, life can open up doors that would bring about unfathomable wealth for you. Besides a seed of prayer and a gift of forgiveness is one of the fastest ways to recovery from hurts and pains. This is the reason the bible says to pray for those who hurt you. There is no point staging revenge or cursing people. Doing this is a sign of a root of bitterness and unforgiveness. True love does not seek the fall of others, neither does it harbour unforgiveness. Rather it releases people and pushes them into their destiny. It encourages them to be all God has for them.

More so, seeking revenge is gratifying to the flesh; because it feels good to see those who have hurt, you go through pain, suffer, or fall. True love is not like that, it dies to self continually. True love raises you up, when all else gives way. The refusal to retaliate a wrong is very painful to the flesh, but as you practise this, you learn how to die to the flesh and be alive to the Holy Spirit. At the end of the day, the feeling you get from releasing others out weighs the feelings you get if you revenge. In fact, in releasing others, God's spirit releases fresh blessings into your lives. You would begin to see divine blessings you never knew existed.

Hebrews 10 vs. 30 *"Vengeance is mine, I will repay"*.

More so, the implication of Isaac being constantly bullied by his rivals is that while they prospered, he was unsettled and had to keep moving from one field to the next. Their peace and wealth must have provoked him to envy at some point. However, he declined the invitation; to travel on Envy Lane. Another factor that can devalue your product and service is envy.

Manoeuvre carefully through Envy Lane until you get to a Healthy Zone! A biblical illustration of what envy can do is found in the story of Cain and Abel in Genesis 4. Both of them were brothers from the same house, and both prepared their gifts. While the preparation of one was accepted, the other was not, and envy was the result that ensued. This invariably led to Cain murdering his brother, and this made God angry. Even though God was angry, He still had mercy on Cain and encouraged him to amend his ways.

However, the spirit of envy would not permit Cain to do this. He wanted his brother's benefit, but did not want to pay the price. The spirit of envy will prevent you from seeing the protection and love of God. Cain did not have to commit murder, he chose to. You do not have to take to the life of crime, you have a choice. You can inform your gifts and talents. You can enrich your garden. You can educate your dreams. You can seek for help straight away if necessary. For Cain, if God had not confronted him with death penalty, he might not have repented. Fortunately, when God did, he repented. The result of his actions was not pleasant. If he were to be alive today, he would tell you that he wished he had not killed his brother. If he had a church, he would preach until all the murderers in the city repented!

> **Proverbs 24 vs. 1** *"Do not be envious of evil men, nor desire to be with them"*.

The day Cain remembered to call on God for mercy was the day his deliverance began. God cannot turn His back on a repentant heart! Even the worst of sinners can find forgiveness, if he chooses to repent. The choice is yours. Having considered anger and envy as factors that devalue your market, let us look at the factors that add value to your market.

Temperance:

For you to maintain the value of your product (service), you need to be on Temperance Road. Temperance is defined as a man's ability to manage himself in a manner that will not threaten the values and belief systems of his environment and those within it. In life, there are certain gifts you receive, and are advised to keep at home. There are others you keep in a safe (away from home), and there is one that must never leave your side. It is the one you live (sleep and eat) with, move (go out and come back) with, and display (in public and in private). It is called temperance (self-control). The time you allow it leave you is when you know its true value.

The Holy Spirit is the vehicle that brings this gift to you, and love is the fuel that energises it to run smoothly. If you hold on to temperance, it would add value to your product, and encourage your market to pay the price. This is because temperance would keep you from anger, envy and all other works of the flesh, which can devalue your product.

In addition, the value of any product or service rendered in a place is very much determined by a number of factors including functionality (how well it meets the needs of the people), adaptability (how flexible it lends itself to their ever changing needs), and congruency (how well it blends in with the way of life of the people).

More so, without temperance, your product may be viewed as being threatening (physically, spiritually, emotionally, psychologically, socially, e.t.c). The natural response to anything seen, as being threatening is anxiety; another factor that devalues your product. While aiming to render a good and excellent service, you may come across some customers from the house of perfectionism. That is okay, because you can trust the Holy Spirit to take care of them (satisfy them), if you dare to ask. Isaac's temperance encouraged him to respond positively, even when it was obvious that they were taking undue advantage of him. This eventually got him his desired outcome (Rehoboth). Genesis 26 vs. 22.

Determination:

Determination refers to your decision to refuse to succumb to adverse pressure, especially where you have a desired outcome in mind. More often than not, sound vision (abstract gift) is the fuel that would keep your vehicle of determination moving. Move with determination.

According to the law of nature, friction (resistance) occurs when two masses (bodies) collide or rob off one another (interaction). Life is filled with masses (living and non-living things) that are in constant collision (interaction) with one another, so you are not exempted from this law of nature.

However, the by-product of this collision (interaction) is heat (resistance). If the intensity is high enough, it can ignite a flame; which may be useful or destructive. What this means is that if you (a living thing) actively interact (collide) with your developed seed (non-living thing), you can produce a flame (determination), that can resist the heat (resistance) that may want to devalue your service (harvest). We can see this being illustrated in Isaac's life.

If Isaac gave up on his attempts at digging the well (after being bullied several times), he may never have got to Rehoboth. His determination (refusal to give up) forced his rivals (oppressors) to give in. They were probably fighting for their land (Abraham had been a stranger there, so Isaac was also a stranger there).

However when they saw Isaacs determination and willingness to add value to their land (through his service), they ceased to bully him. This shows that if your service is geared towards contributing positively to people's lives, your determination will serve as a fragrance that will attract their patronage.

Matthew 10 vs. 22

In summary, remember this direction for placing a value on your service in your garden of destiny (expected end):

Stay off Anger Avenue, Manoeuvre through Envy Lane, turn into and remain on Temperance Road, keep moving with Determination and Diligence, until you arrive at your expected end.

Then the value of your service will be high because of the price you have paid for it. Romans 16 vs. 19-20

Packaging And Branding

> **Genesis 2 vs. 19** *"Out of the ground the Lord God formed every beast of the field and every bird of the air, and brought them to Adam to see what he would call them. And whatever Adam called each living creature that was its name".*

You cannot have a market or harvest if any of the preparation or developmental stages of your seed fails to co-operate with the others. The stages must be congruent for growth and harvest to occur.

However, once the desired result has been achieved, the next phase would be to advertise your product to the market. Advertising is a skill independent of your growth process. The school of architecture exposed this truth to me: no matter how good your work is, you run into trouble with your lecturers if you cannot present it well. The same principle applies in any endeavour you undertake. This is especially true for you to persuade others in accepting what you have to offer.

Hence, one of the first things you would learn if you would excel in marketing your gift is the power of presentation. In marketing, poor preparation means poor presentation and poor presentation means poor performance. Good presentation on the other hand leads to successful advertising. So what are the rules that guard advertisement?

God said to me one morning *"A good recipient"* expresses his gratitude by acknowledging the giver. That acknowledgement is a way of advertising the goodness of the giver.

This is the principle of "the good recipient" and this is the principle demonstrated by large companies and companies who help charities. Their goodness is proclaimed and the people are aware of their existence. Good advertising for them.

However, we should not give so people can advertise us; we should give because we love the Lord. Only He can show us how and where to prosper. Isaiah 48 vs. 17. This is not only good for the givers; it favours the recipient as well as it tells every one around that they are a unit worth identifying with and investing in. Once you can get one person to invest in you, and they find your service excellent, you become a good reference they are willing to promote.

As the advert goes out, people's curiosities are awakened, and this prompts them to try out your product. Once they are satisfied, and you maintain your loyalty, the law of geometry then goes to play in your life and business. Be a good recipient, and cheer people on. Good business for you, good business for them, and good business for the future.

How ever, if you do not have the money to advertise yourself to the public, let your gifts and talents do the advertisement for you. Serve people willingly and whole-heartedly for free, and God would eventually make a way for you. A biblical example of this is Jesus. He used His gift, gave what He had and in return, He got the publicity He required to proclaim the gospel. Jesus refrained the leper (who had just been healed), from following Him. He was to go home, show himself to his neighbours, and tell of how much God had done. God gives us gift so that we can use it to proclaim His love for mankind all over the earth. Luke 8 vs. 38-39.

In fact, before you become an evangelist (proclaiming the goodness of God in your neighbourhood and city), some religious leaders advise you to go and share the testimony with others to encourage them in the Christian faith. They need to know that God is still in the business of healing and deliverance. They need to see the manifestation of Luke 4 vs. 18-19. It makes their work easier. **Matthew 8 vs. 3-4**

More so, I remember in 1997, on my nephew's first birthday, my sister asked me to host and entertain the children. I was a bit apprehensive, as I had never done this before. However, I assured my sister that I would do it. The morning before the party, I prayed and hoped God would tell me not to go ahead. He replied and said, *"What you make happen for others, I will make happen for you"*. Then I knew that there was no escape! This propelled me on, and I have since been sowing different seeds since then.

I must confess that ever since I held on to this principle, things have only gotten better for me; in fact, I have seen the tremendous hand of God upon my life like never before. He has permitted certain privileges into my life that only He could have orchestrated.

I actually enjoyed doing (hosting) the children. I saw how easy it was to serve God by making children happy. Many people had been used by God to keep me happy, and now I found myself keeping other people's children happy. This unknowing to me was to form the courage I had several years later to assist with the children's ministry. If I had refused to accept that challenge that day, I may never have had the opportunity to serve God in that capacity. I may never have had this opportunity to serve you in this capacity as well.

> This means that God has already branded you as very good.

Moreover, you should note that without personally appreciating your product, you would not succeed in advertising it. In the beginning, God saw what He made and appreciated them. He then branded everything He made as "very good" after evaluating them. This means that God has already branded you as very good. Do not devalue yourself and do not let others devalue you. Genesis 1 vs. 31.

How about you appreciating your product? How about you packaging your products? How about you engaging in some branding exercise?

PART 3:
The Market And The Blessing

 Genesis 8 vs. 22 *"While the earth remains, seed time, and harvest, cold and heat, winter and summer, and day and night shall not cease"*.

AN EXCELLENT PRODUCT

Leviticus 26 vs. 4 *"Then I will give you your rains in their season, and the land shall yield its increase, and the trees of the field shall yield their fruit"*.

Marketing Your Service

Genesis 1 vs. 31 *"Then God saw everything that He had made, and indeed it was very good. So the evening and the morning were the sixth day".*

Any experienced sales person will testify that you can market anything you have (gift or skill) if you know how. Everything you have can be recycled to generate income for you. What you consider as dung, is food for another living thing. In order words, your refuse becomes a seed for some one's harvest. That is how God designed life; for continuity. There is no waste. To achieve harmony and survival in your environment, you have to trade some of what you have with others. This is marketing.

Marketing is therefore the art of demonstrating the benefits and functionality of a trade, service or product with the intent of exchanging it for monetary satisfaction or other mutual gain. In the course of commanding a commercial return, you would be required to take responsibility for the marketing. This is a service you owe to God and man. There are things God would do for you, and there are things men would do for you, but there are things that you would have to do for yourself. Genesis 2 vs. 19.

Going back to Genesis 1, we read that Adam started naming the things in his surrounding (tending to his garden), and when he saw Eve, he named her as well. The morale of this is that you should take ownership for the marketing of your harvest (and managing those in your care). You have a duty to God to call them by what you want them to be. We know that every thing God created is very good, so if you believe that, then you can name those under you, as God named His creation. There is a saying that *"give a dog a bad name and that is what he will be. Tell him he is good and he'd be your best friend"*!

What are you calling those God has placed in your care? Are you agreeing with what God says about them? How are you marketing your harvest? What are you calling your products? What are you calling your market? Let goodness accompany the output from your garden—the works of your hand and the returns. Goodness attracts God's blessings.

> **Job 22 vs. 21** *"Agree with God and be at peace; thereby good will come to you"*.

However, you may think that you are too old to market your output (harvest). When it comes to God, the Ancient of days, age becomes irrelevant. As long as you make yourself useful, you would have something of benefit to others. This is what you can sell. Trading occurs anywhere, from your bed at home to the market place and social gathering.

Sale is made based on the level of interaction you are prepared to make and your commitment to the market at hand. You just have to keep at it. Marketers would tell you that they work outside official hours, because you do not know at what point your customer would concede to an exchange. The only certain thing is that you are guaranteed of God's assistance in your endeavours. Isaiah 46 vs. 4.

Give your harvest a go, and even if the marketing falls through initially, you would be convinced that you have tried. The key is to keep trying. Surely, God encourages you to stretch yourself. This is how to build enough stamina to stand the pressure required to stand tall in the market place. You would also experience a testimony similar to Abraham. In Genesis 24, God blessed Abraham (empowered him to prosper) in his old age with every blessing—health, wealth, good family, e.t.c. A further prove that your age is irrelevant to God, is Joshua's testimony of his physical gift: **Joshua 14 vs. 11**.

> You are guaranteed of God's assistance in your endeavours.

More so, in Genesis, we can see how God "marketed" his product (woman). After all the hard work of forming her, He admired her and packaged her nicely, before presenting her to Adam (His market). God had paid the price through hard work and preparation to achieve a good presentation. No wonder man (His market), found the product (woman) irresistible! He saw her and immediately prophesized that she would be the "mother of his children". Genesis 2 vs. 22-23.

Dare to see the hand of God in your product and workers. Dare to align your words with God concerning them. Dare to embrace the blessings of God as they reach out to you in the marketplace.

Ecclesiastes 11 vs. 6 *"In the morning sow your seed, and in the evening do not withhold your hand; for you do not know which will prosper, either this or that, or whether both alike will be good"*

The importance of good presentation or advertising and sales cannot be over emphasized. When your advert goes out, your respondents would invariably become your potential customers. God's reward to you for taking time to till your garden (life) and being commercially productive include faithful and loyal customers. You just have to keep doing what you know is right, which includes stretching yourself and breaking bounds; going the extra mile. Good customers do not wait for your garden to thrive; they expect it to be thriving by the time they get to you. **1st Kings 10 vs. 4-8**

Also, people become good customers when they meet good harvest, not good seed, root, shoot or tree. They need to see positive results (good fruits). **1st Kings10 vs. 24**.

Moreso, for your market to stand the test of time you must keep your customers happy; that is when they can remain loyal to you. What can you do to keep them loyal to you? You would need to meet their demands (reasonable expectations). You must also be prepared for difficult customers (those with challenging expectations). 1st Kings 10 vs. 1-3. While you may, not be able to meet all their exhaustive demands, you can ask God to help. These may turn out to be your most rewarding customers. 1st Kings 10 vs. 10.

King Solomon demonstrated his willingness to keep his customers by asking God for a gift and developing it (sowing and praying). He then deployed it for the benefit of his customer (one of them being the Queen of Sheeba). 1st Kings 9 vs. 1-3.
Demanding needs may be classified as psychological, emotional, social, and physical demands. Your ability to meet these needs is determined by a number of factors, based on the nature of service, you render to them, and your relationship with them. The later can be improved by providing good customer care.
Your customer service package should include freebies (seed) like genuine smiles, good compliments, transparency, respecting individualism by your ability to recognise, respect and meet unique demands. This is what makes you a successful entrepreneur. An entrepreneur who would do this is simply one who would strive to improve his service to God and man, wherever he finds himself.

Jesus exemplified this in the numerous exchanges He made with you. He sowed heavy seeds into your lives (gardens) to enrich it, that it may be well with you on earth and in heaven. In return, God gave Him a harvest (Christians—followers with sound doctrine). You (as potential customers of his salvation) have a whole range of demands from physical to psychological and emotional needs. He is the only one that has the potential and has promised to meet them all. He, the greatest entrepreneur rose to the challenge of meeting your needs by trading the following:

His abundance for your lack
His beauty for your ashes
His comfort for your sorrow
His communion for your loneliness
His divinity for your filth
His eternity for your human mortality
His glory for your shame
His health for your place of sickness
His joy for your place of sadness
His kingship for your slavery
His laughter for your tears
His liberty for your oppression
His might for your weakness
His omniscience for your ignorance
His peace for your turmoil
His quiet rest for your turbulence
His riches for your place of poverty
His righteousness for your sins
His strength for your weakness
His triumph for your losses
His ultimate dominion for your suppression
His victory for your failures
His wisdom for your foolishness
His intended glory for you for the illusion the devil created
His Zoe life and light for your death and darkness

At the end of the transaction, it is a win-win deal. You become a better person, enjoy the privileges of the king's child and He becomes your God.

However, to achieve better results with your customers, your workers have to be happy. Avoid taking hasty steps, let God direct you into how you should go about marketing your harvest. In Genesis 24, we see the servants of Abraham asking God for direction, in seeking for a bride for Isaac. (This can be applicable to seeking for distribution channels for your service). Even when the servants saw the answer, they still waited to confirm it was from God. That not only shows their loyalty to Abraham, it also showed that Abraham lived a life that made his servants acknowledge and fear his God. This eliminated eye service.

This goes to show that if you want loyalty from people, whether as an employer, friend, acquaintance, or family, you need to live a life style of godliness. Let those around you know the God you serve and desire to serve Him as well. There is a great reward in working with godly people. Every thing you do together will command great rewards from God.

Psalm 133 vs. 1
While maintaining your current customers, you should open your eyes to see other potential customers that He has already commanded your way. Even when they look small (financially), you should keep providing excellent service to them. You never can tell what lies ahead. This is what Isaac did. Genesis 24 vs. 63. The first thing Isaac saw from afar, were camels, then he saw Rebecca. God has already sent your market (those who would patronise your service). All you need to do is to identify them. Isaac identified his blessing (gift) while working on the field. The morale here is get busy doing something—rise up and improve the quality of your service!

Furthermore, as a visionary, you would demand accountability and transparency from the people you work with. In as much as you demand these qualities, you must also give it to them. Lead by example, and those you work with would emulate you. The servants of Abraham were on an assignment, and when the occasion arose, they responded in the manner Abraham would have. Genesis 24 vs. 26-27.

> God has already sent your market (those who would patronise your service).

How do you manage unfaithful workers who serve you? Here we see God demonstrating His managerial skills in the way He dealt with His workers. He has an excellent record of finishing all He started well. He is highly skilled and versatile in knowledge and unfaithful workers do not hinder His progress. These was demonstrated when He made man and put Him in the garden to work and co-partner with Him. As the senior partner, God designed and built the earth with all the resources required to make it operational. He blessed it—commanded it to respond to man (as His partner). He then went ahead to form man (giving him ability like him—to reign in life). He blessed man—revealing to him the way the earth can respond to him. He completed the transaction by handing the earth over to him.

Genesis 2 vs. 8

When man fell, He did not sack him, He only altered his job description and relocated him to a place where he would be forced to value and acknowledge His sovereignty and co-operate with Him. From then, man was forced to take a decision to succeed or languish in pain and turmoil. The result meant he now had to work extra hard to lay hold of what was already his. Genesis 3 vs. 24.

Move beyond the ashes and pains of the challenging market. Approach the market as though you have already won them. Make the best of your difficult customers and earn their loyalty.

Your Fallow Season

Leviticus 26 vs. 35 *"As long as it lies desolate it shall rest – for the time it did not rest on your Sabbaths when you dwelt in it".*

L ife was designed by God to reflect His character and expectations from man. Everything about God demonstrated that he is a balanced ruler. He is stable and consistent in all his ways. When He formed the earth, He designed it for man to cultivate. To achieve balance, He recommended that the cultivated land should be allowed to rest after a period. Prolonged cultivation results in the law of diminishing return, and the soil begins to loose its strength. The effect of this is that it does not produce as much as it should and one is advised to leave the soil alone for a number of years. This is the fallow period.

The fallow season in your garden is the periods when you take stock, re-evaluate your gift and service, and look for ways of improving on what exists (your product). It is also the period when you have the tendency to let down your guards, relax and enjoy the proceeds from your service. This is a vulnerable moment for you as well because the enemy is aware of your tiredness. Never underestimate the enemy (even at your weakest moments). A biblical example of how the enemy attacks in the moment of vulnerability is found in 1st kings 3 vs. 16-27.

Remember the two women in the days of King Solomon. There was a famine in Israel; and the people became extremely weak and tired. One of the women; in a moment of weakness; suggested to the other that they take turns in killing each other's child for food. In other words, that was her own vision or solution to the problem!

In a moment of vulnerability, the second woman agreed, both got filled and came back to their senses. As soon as it was time for the visionary of the idea to surrender her own, friction began, and the matter had to be resolved in the King's palace.

The visionary kept her child, but her companion (follower) lost hers, all because she allowed the enemy to take advantage of her vulnerability. Pray! No one is exempted from these moments of vulnerability, pray that God gives you the grace to take a stand (no matter how faint or feeble you feel) at such moments. Let us analyze the visionary's solution to the national problem: of famine.

Firstly, this solution was an immediate one, with no long-term plans. This is a classic example of methods embraced by many societies today; short term plans with no thought for the future — theirs and their children. Secondly, this solution could not have been from God, because prior to that, there had been famine in Israel. Nowhere and on no account did God instruct anyone to eat human beings!

Now because this idea or vision was not from God, unity of spirit could not exist. Therefore, what looked like a proper agreement was actually a verbal agreement with no spiritual consent (willful consent). That is the reason why the bible encourages you to give and accept willing offerings. One would always encounter problems with anything that is given or taken forcefully from God's children (in particular), because it was not done from a willing heart. Both the giver and receiver cannot receive God's blessings. These include ill gotten wealth and wealth gotten through exploitation.

The same applies for those entering into any form of contract or agreement (business, marriage, e.t.c) with other people. Make sure your spirit, soul (mind) and body is at rest before you go into any form of partnership. God encourages unity with the brethren, for this is where your blessings lie.

Another thing you need to do in the face of vulnerability is to surround yourself with the right companion. Those who have little or no regard for their seed (gift) or garden (life), have a way of demotivating those around them. Either you influence them or they influence you.

1st Corinthians 15 vs. 33

You should not be caught hanging about (physically, emotionally, financially, mentally, e.t.c) with people with the wrong kind of jobs (negative visions) or with no jobs (vision). Negative vision is characterised by works of the flesh. They will destroy you and your potentials, by making you trade your gift or vision from God with the devils. Do not take up "the devil's assignment". God does not assign any mark for that. How ever, if you have the right kind of job (vision), you would be too busy for God to engage in demonic products from an evil garden. **Galatians 5 vs. 19-21.**

More so, your fallow season (moment of vulnerability) should not be a moment where you allow your words to be inconsistent with your speech. It should be the time to ensure that the words of your mouth tallies with the word of God and the work of your hands. That is the only way you would get godly outcomes, with no sorrow. **Hosea 10 vs. 12**.

However if you have accidentally taken hasty decisions in moments of vulnerability and later found yourself in compromising situations, take heart. God is still in charge. He

> God encourages unity with the brethren, for this is where your blessings lie.

is a presiding judge with attoneys (intercessors). Everything was created by the power of his word. In the beginning, He created the perfect environment (garden) for man through his word. When man fell, it was the word He spoke that brought relief to man. The nakedness of man brought discomfort; and the covering of God brought some relief. The discomfort in your garden can be eliminated by the power of the spoken word (through prayers). **Isaiah 51 vs. 3**

Wait on the Lord for comfort and beauty. Look to the Lord for increase and prosperity. Be still and experience the joy of the Lord.

Your Future Market

Leviticus 26 vs. 10 *"You will have such a surplus of crops that you will need to get rid of the leftovers from the previous year to make room for each new harvest".*

Having learnt the art of production, there is the need to make provision for the future. Man's insatiable wants mean that his demands would vary with time. Consequently, there must be a contingency plan in place, if you are to keep up with these growing demands. Some form of continuity must be introduced to ensure your garden remains in business for years to come. If you have not discovered how to be in business for a long time, ask God to show you how.

In Genesis, God gave Israel a survival plan through Pharaoh's dream. Joseph gave the interpretation. This plan preserved humanity when famine arose in Egypt. Not only would your garden blossom, it would provide an aura of serenity that would encourage fellowship. In the midst of famine, Egypt attracted Joseph's family. It was a happy reunion and fellowship. Leviticus 26 vs. 5.

How can you keep up with the future market? How can the fruit from your garden stand the test of time and still reproduce long after you have transcended the earth? How can the generations to come benefit from your service and thank God for your life? What you want to achieve with God is a life that people would evaluate now and after, and want to improve on. Nothing lives forever, so to try to achieve eternity by your might would lead to futility. There is a time for you to live and achieve a glorious destiny in God. This is the time you make your contributions to the world. There is also a time for people to bid one another goodnight. **Ecclesiastes 3 vs. 1**.

No one can get hundred percent pass mark with men, you can strive and get excellent mark though. Whatever you do would always be improved upon. That is how God designed life. The only thing that cannot be improved upon is the word of God, because God cannot improve Himself. To improve yourself, ask the Holy Spirit to inspire you and show you how to think. He would give you divine ideas (seeds) that would positively affect your generation and provoke generations to come to continue from where you stopped.

More so, fresh ideas (seeds of destiny) would ignite the flames of research. Since the spirit of God is one, He would lead you to those He wants to be stand with you, as you challenge normalcy.

You would not accept and copy everything you see. You and your team would begin to investigate it thoroughly, find out how and why it works, and what would make it not work, and if there are other ways of improving on it.

More so for you to be succeed, you must cultivate the habit of sharing your knowledge, do not be afraid to share it. As you share your knowledge and brainstorm with people, more ideas (seed) are introduced to your brain. Infact there are some ideas that need to get out of your system, so you do not experience reversal of fortune! **Proverbs 27 vs. 17**.

'I prayed for a God idea and it never came'! You may say. That may appear true, but it's not. You need to know what is yours and believe that some how it would work for you, not against you. When God blessed man in the beginning, that empowerment was intellectual. It referred to his ability to apply his mental capacity to his garden (surrounding) and co-operate with The word (of God). I get stuck a lot, but when I pick my bible, my brain feels refreshed with new ideas, not strange ideas.

I can remember my dad always telling me that I have fantasy ideas. Fantasy is when you do not know how the glorious picture you imagine can be made real. Somehow, by my standing on the word of God, I see how to get what I want—narrow is the way! Life is not with out its challenges; and God never promised us a challenge free life. Infact, the brain is stimulated to produce more when it is exposed to challenging tasks. Treat your knowledge as a seed for your generation and the coming ones. You are guaranteed to be covered and governed by the principle of seedtime and harvest.

Genesis 8 vs. 22

In addition, seed of knowledge always multiplies throughout the generations. Our generation is more comfortable today because previous generations dared to sow seeds of knowledge. Adam and Eve wore fig leaves then; today we wear clothes made from plant and animal based products. The earliest man lived in caves, but today, we live in houses made of bricks, stones, and mortar. As you are diligent in improving your service, your fame would spread wide and far, and "Queens of Sheba"—investors; would begin to look for you and bless you. They would also provide you with all the resources you need to improve. **Isaiah 45 vs. 14**

This would include people exploring the output from your garden. They would realise that you are not only a blessing to yourself; you are also a blessing to your society and the coming generation. This is what the word of God promised. Our leaders testified to it, and we saw it work for generations; try it for yourself as well. You can not trust God and go wrong.

> Seed of knowledge always multiplies throughout the generations.

It is a known thing that God has given every society the seed (mental, and human) resources they need to progress. As you begin to harness and improve the output from your garden, aspiring nations would gravitate towards you. This is because they realise that a society that will lead is one that will encourage and pump money into research. They have come to realise that although it is good to pump money into the other forms of resources, the one that does not suffer from the law of diminishing returns is the mental resources (the brain).

The more you exercise the brain to think, the more creative it gets. In addition, the human brain functions in a similar way for someone in the North Pole, as it does for the person in the South Pole, though they may behave differently and differ in biological form.

However, they would function in similar ways if exposed to the same condition (environmentally and psychologically). Today, we have different parts of the body being transferred from one person to the other, through the power of research. Tomorrow, God may permit man to acquire the knowledge and expertise to transfer brain from a dying person to preserve the life of another. You can be that man or woman that would make the difference in the world. You can be that child that would dare to work on your idea and wipe the tears off the faces of other children.
The positive work you contribute would be documented over the years, and like a baton, the knowledge can be passed onto the next generation. What this means is that through the spirit of unity or team work generations can progress on the work, without having to waste time re-inventing the wheel. Our fathers told us and that is why we know what we know today.

More so in Genesis 1, God created the earth and its occupants and in Isaiah 45 vs. 18, we are told that He did not create it in chaos. He created it so we can all live in it, there is room for every one. Man, being formed in God's image, received the baton of creativity and continued the work of development (technological advancement). With this in mind, you may still come across complexities with your ideas. Go back to God in prayers and rest in Him. Relax in Him and learn to enjoy His presence; remember He did not ask you to seek Him in vain. As you seek Him for solutions, you would find Him. Do not forget, the innovations we see today are the results of the complexities that has been generated through researches carried out over the generations.

Knowledge is a gift or seed and the truth is that there is no new wheel. It is in breaking down the complexities of life that you find irregularities within the system. This would more often than not, provoke you to begin to search for answers— undiscovered truths.

If you would therefore be a good conduit of exchange for research you would take time out to study the system and its complexities, break it down (through analysis), and relay it to the recipient, in the process they can digest.

Lastly, we know that every society has all it needs to solve its problems. The ones that seem to be advancing swiftly are those who have decided to study life, understand how it was formed, measure it against its functions, observe the loopholes, and find solutions to the anomalies. Of course, this solution always brings in wealth for whoever unveils the undiscovered truth.

Do your best to be productive. Strive to go beyond normalcy. Make room for futuristic demands.

The Cheaper
Way For Staying
In Business

> **Ephesians 3 vs. 17** *". . . That Christ may dwell in your hearts by faith; that ye, being rooted and grounded in love may have power to comprehend with all the saints what is the breathe and length and height and depth . . . ."*

As earlier mentioned, if you would succeed in marketing your service, you must place a value on it. The value you place must be such that it brings in maximum profit at minimum cost. This is the only way that you would remain in business for a long time. So how do you achieve this godly fate (maximum profit at minimum cost) with your market?

If the tree of your garden (life) is firmly fixed to the soil called love, a fruit of faith is produced that would lead to the harvest called Christ. Christ is an entrepreneur that cannot fail. With this business guru, you can achieve your fate. The slave masters of old took a cue from Him. Think of your future market, and stop the fish business! So what is the fish business?

The fish business is the story of the slave masters and their captives. We may argue that they prepared and delivered all they said that they would. In return, they captured slaves as a reward for their generosity. Good business people! A good businessperson is one who works with profit in mind. They must have taken their cue from God in the bible times, though not all of them were christians. Proverbs 8 vs. 10-11. We may also argue that the deliveries were good and functioned well. So what went wrong? How did the business become fish business!

Did the recipients of the wheels fail to fully grasp and understand the modus operandi. Did the baton of knowledge that was once firmly gripped on receipt, become loose in the hands of the successors? Did the baton drop from their hands with the progress of time? Maybe the deliveries became exposed to abuse because of the growing needs of the people. Unplanned futuristic incidentals definitely posed a strain on the system and caused it to suffer a tear. Obviously whatever tear was experienced has been stitched and the wounds healed, but the scar remains.

Today, like others who would love to see you succeed, I challenge you to embrace godly knowledge; not just for your time but also for the future generation. Challenge your intellectual capacity. It is absurd and unproductive to ponder over the past, leave it alone and begin to challenge your present and tomorrow. **Proverbs 24 vs. 3-4**.

More so, the downside to grabbing the wheels without mastering how it functions is that it would not function optimally. If it does, it would be a high maintenance venture. This is because you would either go back to the manufacturers of the wheel, pay them large sums of money to come in and maintain the wheel you grabbed from them or you would have to master how it works. In both cases, you would be spending unnecessary resources (time or money) that could have been avoided. Morale — If you are a trainee, master the system before you demand for your freedom so you do not waste resources (time and money) reinventing the wheel! You are one of the gardens God created with unique abilities. There are other gardens that He uses to achieve other purposes, which your garden may not achieve.

However, if you are going to continue leaning on other people's fish scheme, you must be prepared to spend your resources (time, intellect, money) on them. Now in the spirit of business, they would give you fish in exchange for your service (life). Keep away from the fish business, and strive to achieve a win-win situation for you both.

If you want to operate in the true spirit of business, while you are trainee, borrow as many skills as you can. Learn, master them, and be confident. Then you can tap into the spiritual for divine assistance in breaking away. When you break away, you can stand shoulder to shoulder like partners and not like a dependant. Then you can compete with one another, help one another, and finally together you can help the less privileged and generations to come.

However, I am not suggesting that servant hood is bad. It is a good system as it affords you the opportunity to learn from other people. It becomes bad, when no plan is in place for progression. This is God's way of dealing with His children. Remember the story of Isaac and Esau? Isaac had just been deceived into pronouncing a blessing over Jacob, instead of Esau. The prophesy was that Esau would serve Jacob. However, when Esau pleaded (prayed earnestly) with Isaac and begged for a blessing, heaven intervened. Isaac prophesized that at an appointed time, Esau would become restless and break the yoke of slavery off his neck. Then Esau would become a free man once again. **Genesis 27 vs. 40**, **Genesis 33 vs. 9**.

God blessed every seed of Abraham, those who remained under the curse were the ones who strayed away from the covenant. As a child of God, eternal slavery is not your portion. Serve people, learn from them, and proceed to help others. Then there is continuity, then there is progress and then there is a boost in the morale of the people.

Another down side to the fish business is that you put yourself in the position where you can be easily trampled. This is not being humble; it is wrongly applying the right type of knowledge. Be on the lookout for the basic raw materials that your garden needs to thrive well. Settle down and learn the tending techniques, be comfortable with the garden equipments and get to work. You would in turn maximise your output, experience exponential growth and have enough increase to command commercial returns. Every progress is a by-product of hard work and determination. There are loads of opportunities out there. All you have to do is to identify the one that is yours, grab it and commit it to God.

More so, it is a known fact that wealth is made by meeting the demands of a challenge. Many businesses have been built on the bedrock of this theory — providing solutions to the complexities of life. You can be rest assured that the challenges you decide to handle and proffer solutions to, would put you in a confronting stance with your counter parts. Some insist that it's either you kill them or they kill you — put your garden out of use!

You need to hold onto your garden (life), until the Lord calls you home. To attempt to pack up is to attempt to fail. Remember God created you to rule your world. Your contemporaries want you to succeed. They need to know that you are not intimidated, because they know their limits and weaknesses. The next time the contender steps into your garden make sure you have an equivalent in your store! Your contender needs to be aware that they can turn to your God in their hour of need. Look at what is available to your garden and get working. This is evangelism.

More so, realise that more money can be realised from a system of government that works. Your input is needed, and this is a sub conscious fact that every contender knows but is afraid to admit. This is why you need to contend with wisdom. Some die in battle, while others live on. Some get to the finish line dead and some finish strong and keep smiling. What pattern of result are you expecting from your garden? There are yet some contenders whose main aim of trying to put your garden out of business is so you can open avenues for more varieties. Ponder on these and push harder — you cannot leave the race. You can not stop your garden from being fruitful. Even if you decide to stop your garden from agriculture produce, and embrace architecture, you may discover that it is easier and cheaper to plant a seed in the soil and nurture it than to erect a garden shed!

Since our God is a resourceful God, nothing is wasted in His hands. If you need to recycle your business and turn it into one that would glorify God, ask Him and He would show you how. When God prospers you, you would not need to surrender to fish business.

Besides, all your competitors would realise the hand and grace of God on you and would allow your unique blessing to thrive. They may attempt to compete with you, but your unique grace would help you stand out. In Ruth 4, the man that was meant to marry Ruth wanted her husband's property but not the responsibility attached. Maybe he did not have the grace to handle it. **Ruth 4 vs. 6**.

Periodically, the fish business is a complex business we all fall into subconsciously. It is either you are negotiating to pull yourself down and out; or you are pulling someone else down and out. None of these adds value or increase to any society. Neither does any of this command the blessings of God. What God blesses is communal fellowship in the society, regardless of who you are. You need a win—win situation to maintain a cheap business.

Although Boaz had all the resources, he required to marry, his character made him respect his people. He did not have to strangle them or kill them in order to marry Ruth. If he did, no one would have attended the marriage ceremony, let alone the naming ceremony of his son. No one would be around to encourage him. **Ruth 4 vs. 11**

More over, there is a popular saying that the apple on the other side is always greener. Well this may or may not be true, depending on how much work you are willing to put into your garden of apples. Cultivate your garden well, and it would blossom with time. Some past leaders have not adequately

> Since our God is a resourceful God, nothing is wasted in His hands.

supported their people in terms of development, and today their children are being faced with the giants their fathers refused to kill.

So there fore begin to fight the giants that your predecessors have refused to fight. Fight the giants that have the potential to extradite your children. Fight the giant that is not cost effective to you or your children.

Thanking The Lord Of The Harvest

Jeremiah 31 vs. 12 *"They will come home and sing songs of joy on the heights of Jerusalem. They will be radiant because of the many gifts the Lord has given them-the good crops of wheat, wine, and oil, and the healthy flocks and herds. Their life will be like a watered garden, and all their sorrows will be gone"*.

We have looked at how a man can discover, harness and deploy his gifts. One of the blessings of God upon a hardworking person is the promise of a joyful harvest. It is the kind of harvest that brings fulfilment. If you dare to go out there and sow your seed in the market place (where you work), at the agreed time, your reward would come. Every worker; whether salaried or wages, look forward to a paycheck; the reward from work done in accordance to a given contract. It is a thank you from the authority, which gladdens the heart of the recipient. Thanksgiving is a response to a reward appropriately given.

As God gives you a joyful harvest, you are expected to thank Him. It gladdens His heart and encourages him to do more for you. This is the reason why we must endeavour to thank Him for everything — the seed, the soil, the garden tools, the rain, the growth process, and the harvest. One thing that must be noted is this, if God does not bless (empower you to prosper) or permit your increase, all efforts would be wasted. Most times thanksgiving is expressed in terms of offering. 1st Corinthians 3 vs. 6-8.

Although God is responsible for the growth, we need to take ownership for our offering to Him. In Genesis 19, Abraham made an offering to God; and took responsibility to ensure that the offering was intact. God saw the vultures, but did not do anything about it. If Abraham did not send the vultures away, they would have eaten his sacrifice and he would not have been able to offer it to God. There are ravengers that destroy harvest and affect your thanksgiving. You owe it to yourself to remain tuned into God so you can have a joyful harvest. 1st Corinthians. 3 vs. 11.

Another person that took ownership of his thanks giving was the father of the prodigal son in Luke 15. Like a lost gift that was restored, his son was restored to him. The father (visionary)'s response was not of anger, but of joy that his boy (or gift) had returned home. In fact, before the boy (gift) opened his mouth, his father was overjoyed. The bible says that as soon as the father sighted his son from a distance, he made up his mind to be joyful. He commanded the servants to prepare a sacrifice of thanks giving, not even his second son could stand in the way.

This should be your response to any of your gifts you identify from a distance. It could be the seed God may decide to use to propel you greater heights that you never imagined. You need to welcome it with thanksgiving to God. Create an atmosphere of joy in your mind. Your gift should come and meet you at home rejoicing. If it does not find joy and appreciation, it may decide to leave again.

An atmosphere of peace and joy is where creativity is birth. If you fail to discern your gift from afar (capture it in your mind), it may not materialise. Thanksgiving exposes your gift and creates the strength to develop it. **Luke 15 vs. 21-24**. More so, like the prodigal son's brother, there would be other emotions that would try and frustrate your joy and discourage you from giving thanks to God. If they arise, stand your ground, stake your claim, take ownership for your joy, and watch as your gift remains with you. **Luke 15 vs. 25-30.** As earlier stated, your gifts can be converted into a blessing with the right attitude (if you are willing to harness it). It was the father's (visionary's) attitude of gratitude that enabled the prodigal son (gift) to take his position as his son (bless him).

Wherever you are, if you belong to God, remember this, it is not God's desire that you die without fulfilling your purpose. Why don't you create an attitude of gratitude around you, so God can help make your gift manifest.

> An atmosphere of peace and joy is where creativity is birth.

Be a blessing to God. Be a blessing to yourself. Be a blessing to your world.

Look Out For The Garden Watchers

Ezekiel 3 vs. 16 *"Now it came to pass at the end of seven days that the word of the Lord came to me, saying, Son of man, I have made you a watchman for the house of Israel; therefore hear a word from my mouth, and give them warning from me".*

Earlier chapters dealt with sowing, nurturing and marketing your seed under the influence of the Holy spirit. However, we can not do this in isolation of the garden watchers. Who are they? They are the watchmen, that are in charge of your spiritual growth. Planting is an art that is guided by spiritual laws and forces. Without heaven responding with rain, wind and the sun, the effort may be futile. The same applies to every aspect of human growth – physical, spiritual, intellectual, e.t.c.

Although you have direct access to God, there are yet those who God has given permission to look watch over you while you sleep or work. They can access information, that can be used to guide you from the spiritual realm when your guards are down. They are also gardens that have been well watered by God, their fruits is what we see that makes us realise the hand of God upon them. So although we are all labourers, they have been picked by God to watch over you. They are your garden watchers. **1 Corinthians 3 vs. 9**.

You cannot have a bumper harvest without your garden watchers.

You can have something else! God put them to watch over you, and put you in your field to cater for them from your increase.

In 1997, I remember the Holy Spirit used the story of the widow of Zarephath and the Shunamite woman to encourage me in the area of sowing. I decided to study both women and found out that

1) They both looked after the man of God (Elijah and Elisha) that was sent into their lives. **1st Kings 17 vs. 8-9, 2nd Kings 4 vs. 8-10**

2) They both had a son. **1 Kings 17 vs. 12, 2nd kings 4 vs. 17**

3) The Widow's son died and God intervened **1st Kings 17 vs. 22**

4) The Shunammite woman's son developed a sudden illness (11 kings 4 vs. 18) and before the man of God could appear, he had died. **2nd Kings 4 vs. 32**

5) Their action (faith) however restored their sons.

6) These were women who had needs, yet they obeyed God. It was in the place of their obedience to God that He met them at the point of their needs by the power of the spoken word, through the men of God – the garden watchers. This is the reason why it is good to be discerning and recognise when God sends people your way.

Remember to look after the garden watchers because they are ministers of God. A garden watcher is an intercessor. We are all chosen by God to be garden watchers, just that some receive signals at a higher frequency than others. Those whose antennas are very sharp are those God has chosen to draw nearer, so they can perform better. These are the ones in full time ministry. They cover the tracks that your natural abilities may not cover because while you may neglect the signals you receive, they dare not.

Any intercessor, whom God has given the privilege to see into the spirit, would tell you that there are many things happening in that realm, and some cannot be uttered! As a garden watcher, who is not in full time ministry (because of work or study), you may not have the energy and time required to pray as much as those in full time ministry. The full time garden watchers see possibilities and negotiate on your behalf. This is the reason they deserve to be looked after.

In Leviticus, though the Levites were not given any inheritance, the Israelites were commanded to help meet their needs. Their responsibility was to look after the things of God and be fed off God's house. They were not to concern themselves with the business of the world for God separated them to Himself. **Numbers 8 vs. 19, Numbers 18 vs. 20-21, Numbers 18 vs. 24**

More so, when you sow into people's lives, you place a demand on the source of their lives (God). He was the one that asked you to care for them. Take your focus away from men and look onto God.

It is possible that in times past, people might have taken undue advantage of your generosity. If they are unfaithful to you, the God who made them and commanded you to bless them is not. He will surely bring your reward in due season.

> He will surely bring your reward in due season.

Look out for your garden watchers. Make your resources available for their needs. Let God turn your seed to a bumper harvest.

Look Out For Your Brethren

> **Leviticus 19 vs. 9-10** *"When you reap the harvest of your land, you shall not wholly reap the corners of your field, nor shall you gather the gleanings of your harvest. And you shall not glean your vineyard, nor shall you gather every grape of your vine yard, you shall leave them for the poor and the stranger: I am the Lord your God"*.

Part of sowing into the lives of others includes looking out for fellow labourers in the vineyard, not only the garden watchers. Not every labourer would be rich, and not every one of them would have direct or easy access to their needs. God always encourages you to be sensitive to them. Your responsibility is to harvest, and make allowance for labourers that are not as opportune as you. This is not saying that you should encourage laziness or slothfulness. There are those with genuine needs who would need your support periodically. **Ezekiel 36 vs. 8.**

Fellow labourers include your colleagues in the market place, your brethren in the church, and everyone you share a common goal. They are positioned by God to strengthen your hands and the hands of others. They can give you seeds (ideas) from their garden. They come from God although they may be of diverse background.

Galatians 6 vs. 10. As earlier discussed, when Joseph got to the palace, he did not forget his brothers. As soon as he discovered that they had a need, he reached out and helped them. They saw their brethren in need and decided to rise to the occasion, following the command God gave to the children of Israel.

In addition, the reason God commanded you to look out for your fellow labourers is because in the beginning God created them to have dominion like you. They realise that they were meant to be like you. When the devil came with sin and all manner of maladies (oppression, obsession, possession and affliction), it deprived some of them of the ability to regain that level of dominion. To encourage them in the journey through life, He put you in strategic locations to help meet their needs. **Leviticus 25 vs. 35**

There are some that have to live their comfort zone including families just to make ends meet. These are the ones that leave their home, their people, their environment and even what they know, in order to meet a need. It may be that work colleague from "another planet", or continent speaking a different language to yours. It may be that brethren from another faith trying to settle in with yours. It may just be that traveller that has just been defrauded and needs help finding his bearing.

All these are co labourers that are potential victims of oppression. You can do something. You can make that colleague's job easier by making up your mind to be nice and contribute to the success of the work environment. You can help that brother from a different faith see God as a loving father. You can assist that lost traveller by showing her the way out of her predicament or referring her to the appropriate authorities. **Leviticus 25 vs. 17** The four lepers were also men, who rose from rags to riches and did not forget their brethren. In fact, they knew that if they do not go and look for their brethren, it might not be well with them. **2nd Kings 7 vs. 8-9**

Another biblical illustration of looking out for others is found in Joshua 1 vs. 13-15. This is the principle God gave to Joshua when the Israelites were going to possess their inheritance. Although certain tribes got their inheritance first, they could not eat of its produce until everyone was sorted. **Joshua 1 vs. 13-15** The size of your proceeds does not matter, what matters is how you are able to influence the kingdom of God with it (via helping others). You should leave enough knowledge (the ones at your disposal) for the next generation to proceed. Be a good sportsman, pass the baton well. It is when christians begin to do this that the spirit of unity can thrive. Unbelieving Christians and non christians can see the force of unity, and the love that emanates from here will attract them. For in the atmosphere of unity, love abides.

> You should leave enough knowledge for the next generation to proceed.

If you do not do what you are meant to do in your generation, God would not break His covenant. Like He did for the children of Israel, He will simply look for another labourer that can

do the job and co-operate to establish His purpose on earth.
Jeremiah 31:34

If this scripture would be fulfilled, we must ask ourselves, whether it would be in this generation or the next. I have made up my mind that the scripture would be fulfilled in my lifetime and that I would align myself for the fulfilment of the scripture.

I am a labourer and have taken my place. We are waiting for you to take your place. Then we can wait on others as they take their place as co labourers.

Monopoly

Ezekiel 31 vs. 8-9 *"This tree became taller than any of the other cedars in the garden of God. No cypress had branches equal to it; no plane tree had boughs to compare. No tree in the garden of God came close to it in beauty. Because of the magnificence I gave this tree, it was the envy of all the other trees of Eden, the garden of God".*

Having gained mastery over your market, present and future, there is need to be careful, so you do not build a prison (for yourself) that would antagonise the purpose of God on earth. When you have been through the cycle of sowing, reaping and successful marketing, you would stand tall and be the envy of others. God's purpose is for you become a divine advert to show forth His glory. It is not for your own glory. He needs to show others what is possible, if they can dare to follow Him. **Isaiah 60 vs. 1.** Monopoly is a complete control of a trade, product, or service run by a person or a unit of the society. The spirit of monopoly suggests you look to one system of governance for your wellbeing. It suggests a form of control or dominion, and while this sounds and feels good, if handled poorly can end up being devastating.

Monopoly is good when there is the need to prove your uniqueness in a market. You can push a trade, service or product into the market or take it away through this means. It is useful where there is need for development in a system. When others are dragging their feet, you can force them to buckle up by threatening their service, product or trade. God has called you to a life of uniqueness and holiness. He has called you to be distinguished, so you can take a stand for him. He has made you a well-watered garden so you can encourage others.

More so, you can achieve monopoly that is divine by going to God and asking Him to show you how. As mentioned earlier in this book, God can not bless you outside your knowledge. He uses what you have to bless you. For example, it is not possible for a banker to perform an operation in a hospital theatre, and end up getting the price for an outstanding performance, unless he goes through the appropriate training. Infact it would be a criminal offence.

Also you are not the commander of the excellence in your life, but God. Your responsibility is to arise and do something that God can distinguish. Take time to discover one of your gifts, as discussed earlier, harness it and develop it. Sow your seed, nurture it, and watch (and pray for excellence) it grow. Let God distinguish your garden. There is nothing that you cannot use to break grounds. Look at the fashion industry. Some of the latest trends are accepted today because someone went behind the scene, bent her back and allowed God open her eyes to see creative ways of expressing excellence through fabrics.

The motive behind monopoly is to force people to accept change, where the pioneer thinks the people need a change of governance. God left you and I in the world with a choice of life and death. In His mercy, when he sees you straying, he may at times introduce you to a system of governance that would force you to change your mind.

However, where there is monopoly, deception cannot be over ruled. The decisions taken by this singular unit are solitary and may be utilitarian. Where the power of the unit transcends the environment they influence, oppression becomes the order of the day and deception becomes prevalent. A biblical example of what deception can lead to is found in the story of Isaac and his sons. Isaac had become deem in discernment. He had sent his first son, Esau to get him a meal so he can eat it and bless him before passing away.

His wife eaves dropped on the conversation and altered the intention. She felt Jacob should have been the first, so she engineered Jacob to grab his brother's birth right. They succeeded through the monopoly of Rebecca, Isaac's wife. The funny thing is that where there is manipulation, the victim always senses it and at times lets his deceiver get away with it. When Jacob presented the meal, Isaac made an interesting remark and said, "*I hear the voice (lovely and persuasive speech) of Jacob, but I feel the hand (works) of Esau*". **Genesis 27 vs. 22**. Although Isaac's discernment was getting deem, his intuition told him the right thing, but his feelings prevailed. This is what deception does, it tries to appeal to your feelings, until you disregard your intuition, (a gift God has given you to guard against the deception of the enemy). Ephesians 5 vs. 6

Like the bible said, the glory of God is the reason why you would be distinguished. If the trees in your garden are to become symbols of excellence, it is for the glory of God. History has a record of well-known and powerful leaders, who embraced monopoly and later became extremely perverse. Most of them stated out humble and sincere, but may be they later forgot the source of their victories and began to deceive people. **Romans 1 vs. 28.** They failed to be accountable to God and man, and so when they went off target, there was no one close enough to pull them back on track. They became isolated and left alone in their own world. The devil discovered this, and the aftermath of their tenure was disastrous to the human race. Such is the fruit we get when we neglect the word of God in our lives, and society. This is what monopoly can do if not properly handled.

Proverbs 18 vs. 1

The strategy the devil used on them was the winning strategy God gave to Joshua in Joshua 8 vs. 3-8. If you can lure the enemy away from his comfort zone, then you would be able to defeat him in no time. If the devil can convince you to leave your garden uncultured, in no time, the seed you pains takingly planted would die off.

More so, we would discover that most of the principles the devil uses are actually principles that God had given His children in the bible. All the devil does is to capitalise on a man's neglect to study the word of God. The Holy Spirit tells you what is available to you to help you remain on track. We thank God today that the church of God has woken up and is realising her place in the society. We are taking back everything the devil has stolen from us. We would no longer forsake the gathering of the brethren, nor would we refute sound Christian doctrines. **Job 15 vs. 8**? When you are alone in your garden, God would make divine provision available to you. However, being a relational God, there would also come a time when He would encourage you to begin to interact with other gardeners. This is so that you can cover one another's back (benchmarking).

A good example is the Israelites in the wilderness. While they were alone in the wilderness, God provided for them supernaturally. More over as soon as they left the wilderness, the manner ceased. They had to relate with others in order to have their needs met. **Joshua 5 vs. 12.** In this way, power was decentralised and every one looked up to God, as opposed to man.

> The Holy Spirit tells you what is available to you to help you remain on track.

Arise and strive to be the best that you can be now. Let your spirit key into God's wisdom. Make monopoly a tool for positive change today.

Alas!
The Competitors

Ezekiel 36 vs. 30 *"I will give you great harvests from your fruit trees and fields, and never again will the surrounding nations be able to scoff at your land for its famines".*

Where there is monopoly, there are bound to be competitors. These may consist of those whom you may have trained (helped) in times past and even those who have forcefully grabbed the wheels from you. Acknowledge them, for where there are no competitors, the drive to improve might not be strong. As long as God is for you, you cannot go out of business. God would continue to prosper you. When the competition is fierce and you feel strangled, God can miraculously deliver you. Proverbs 2 vs. 21.

For you to accept the challenge to compete, you must know what it means and what it takes to compete. To compete is to compare oneself or societal unit forcefully with another by words, thoughts or deeds. Competition is necessary for growth to occur. Where there is no competition, the people lack the drive and motivation to live. Competition is a God given ability to aid survival on the earth. All living things, including plants and animal compete for survival. In your garden, there is also competition. From the moment you sow your seed, the seed competes in the soil for survival until it is broken and dies off. The roots compete with other matters in the soil for nutrients and water. The plants and flowers have to contend with the environment. The gardener has to compete in the market place for there to be good sale. Competition occurs throughout life.

To compete and win there are laid down principles. As earlier stated, in a game of chess, you follow the rules of the game as stated in the manual if you want to win. In a similar vein, to win in life, you have to follow biblical principles. To develop a well-nurtured garden, you prayerfully follow the laid down procedure for the seed you desire to plant. Each seed requires a unique care to give the optimal output. Avoid conditions that would adversely impede growth. **Jeremiah 4 vs. 36**. The inability to welcome competition as a positive thing may lead to unpleasantness. Remember King Herod in the bible. Matthew 2 vs. 3-6, Matthew 2 vs. 13, Matthew 2 vs. 16

God announced that a king would be born, and King Herod could not take it. To show that he was not thinking well, he did not even take the time to find out what the nature of this king would be. He probably thought that Jesus was going to overthrow his government on earth. He thought power began and ended with him. What he did not know is that God will always have his way. **Lamentation 3 vs. 37.** All he knew was that a king was about to be born and he could not take it. He could not stand competition, and the only way he could monopolise the throne was to eliminate all the babies under two. Inability to accept competition and the outcome can be as tragic as that. What he refused to acknowledge was the fact that no one can stop the hand of God from moving, when He decides to. Isaiah 43 vs. 13.

More so, your competitors would force you to defend your market. This reminds me of what happens in a design school. Once the instructors guided the students to a certain point, they are expected to produce series of design options prior to their final presentation, and defend it. It is called a crit. The idea behind the crit is this, "If it is your work, prove it to me. Prove to me that it would work. Give me a reason to accept your idea". What it simply means is every new idea would be criticised, and not necessarily in a compassionate way.

Defending your market is also another way of staking your claim in the society. There is a lot of competition out there and you would need to assure people that your market provides them with the best options. The key to surviving the competition out there is to be able to logically and systematically stake your claim. We see a biblical example of these in the daughters of Zelophehad, and the men who had become unclean accidentally.

The daughters of Zelophehad would have lost their inheritance if they had not defended themselves. God commanded that inheritance be given to men of the family only, but this family had only females. They brought

> Likewise, you can bring your request to God and watch Him do the unusual in your life.

their case to God, and got what they wanted. Likewise, you can bring your request to God and watch Him do the unusual in your life.

Finally, in the bible, any one that defiled himself with a corpse was meant to keep away from the pass over. The men that encountered the corpse dared to challenge the law and got what they wanted. **Numbers 9 vs. 6-7, Joshua 17 vs. 3-4.** In all these examples, if the people had failed to defend their rights (ideas), they would not have got what they desired.

See your competitors. Acknowledge your competitors. Challenge your competitors.

Conclusion:
Do Not Become God!

Ephesians 5 vs. 1 *"Therefore be imitators of God as dear children"*.

Earlier chapters have highlighted the effects of deception on your seed and growth. There are however cases where deception is not obvious. In all your quest to discover your gift and harness it, be careful that you do not end up on a side you did not bargain for. You can end up becoming an 'idol' in your field; a god in your own right. It is possible.

However, be careful that you do not take the place of God in your life and in the lives of others. The bible calls us gods, we are to represent Him, as His ambassador but not become Him. To become God is to equate ourselves to Him. It is to ascribe all the glory to ourselves. **Psalm 82 vs. 6**, **2nd Corinthians 5 vs. 20**

What this means is that we are to represent God on earth — walk like Him, talk like Him and work for Him. We are not expected to be Him. For example, can you imagine how preposterous it would be if the ambassador of a country like United States of America goes out and proclaims himself as the country (he represents)? He can say that figuratively. However, if he goes ahead to force it into practice and says to everyone "if you want to dine in the statue of liberty, climb my hands and seat comfortably there", it would not be a pretty story.

There is something innate about man, which seeks for more, and if care is not taken idolatry can step in. Idolatry steps in when there is an abuse of demand on a person or thing. Every one seeks for an extremely dependable, reliable, unshakable personality of good conduct. While the quest is good in itself, it becomes bad if found outside God. By nature, you might have mastered the routine tasks you have been involved in over the years. The demand on you should be high, but when it pushes you to dance to the tune of perfectionism, then you have to beware of the sound track. There is a level of demand that is acceptable and there is a level of demand that is overbearing. If you must dance to any tune of perfection, it should be from the sound track of God's love. Any other sound track would see you heading for the ditch! Colossians 3 vs. 14

However, once you hear the tune of perfectionism, the solution is to become transparent! Let people identify with your strengths and weaknesses so that they can know how to work with you, or if to work with you. Nib every form of insinuations, which suggests that you are superior to others; to the board before it becomes a platform for setting you up. Do not allow anyone make you into what you have not been created to be. Do not allow people make a donkey or monkey out of your life. You are a child of God, made to function like Him, you are not Him. When people begin to criticise and attack you unduly, point them to God. Let them know that He is the only one who does not err. Do not allow them make you leave up to standards that are not humanly realistic.

I am not suggesting that you do not listen and take corrections. I am suggesting that you do your best to meet realistic standards. At every point in time, look around for partners you can bench mark with, look beneath you at how your performance is influencing those coming behind and lastly look up to God for the standard He expects of you. This makes you accountable to God and man.

More so, you may think that people can never make you into a God. Look at King Saul in the bible.

1st Samuel 10 vs. 24. He refused to draw the line between what was his and what was God's. The children of Israel set him up and he danced to their tune. He failed to acknowledge that it is God who gives man ability. 1st Samuel 10 vs. 24. He thought that he had to be the only one to do everything and be the best at everything. It could be argued that he was an ambitious ruler. Now there is nothing wrong with ambition, it becomes demonic when it moves against God. **1st Samuel 18 vs. 7-9**. Playing God causes you to lose focus. The moment King Saul took his eyes off his divine vision (to defend Israel against the enemy); he received another vision (to pursue David — the Lord's anointed). More so, as you become a master, train those who are coming behind you to think and cover your back. Encourage them to have a say in the decisions you make. Remember a leader that would be effective is one that would allow others grow with him. Joshua is an example of a successful leader. In order words, he was not intimidated by what others were going to achieve. **Joshua 17 vs. 14-18, Joshua 18 vs. 8**

Another reason you should be accountable to man, especially when you become a leader in your field can be found in Numbers 13 and 14. Moses had sent the elders of Israel to spy out the land that God had promised to give them. Prior to this, they had experienced the hand of God mightily on several occasions. The leaders went as God had sent them and brought back a negative report. **Numbers 13 vs. 17-20, Numbers 13 vs. 30-32.** Apart from Joshua and Caleb, who were also elders, there was no follower that could open his mouth and talk positive. One thing the Holy Spirit ministered to me on my way to work one morning was this. Leaders need to encourage loyalty from their followers, and followers need to encourage their leaders by applying integrity to their stewardship. **Proverbs 12 vs. 18**

This is not suggesting that people should begin to challenge authority unduely, but to stand as a back up for them. Authority figures are human beings in the forefront of the enemy's attack. Occasionally in the face of strong temptation, they would require the support of their followers. Assuming the children of Israel were loyal to Moses and their leaders, as soon as they received the bad report, some of them should have sensed the weariness in their leaders and risen up to help. They should have encouraged their leaders not to loose heart, but believe in the God that had brought them thus far. Rather they refused to take ownership for their leaders, accepted the report, and allowed the entire race to become disillusioned. **Numbers 14 vs. 1-4.**

The spirit of God must have moved through Joshua and Caleb, and what the followers refused to do, they did. **Numbers 13 vs. 30.** Their failure to enter the promise land was not just the leaders' fault, but also the followers. Good and effective leadership is a by-product of good and effective follower ship. **Numbers 14 vs. 22-24**

In conclusion, I would just like to encourage you to master your skills, be ambitious, but do not become God and don't give people the opportunity to make you one.

Take ownership of your stewardship! Take ownership of your leadership! Take ownership of your blessings!

From Me To You

Proverbs 18:16 *"A man's gift makes room for him and brings him before great men"*.

Have you ever stood before kings?
Would you like to stand before kings?
Do you have what it takes to stand before kings?
Are you prepared to stand before kings?
Do you know that you can stand before kings?

What do you do naturally without supervision?
What can you do without having to put in so much?
What would you do for others, even if you were not paid?
All these are indicators of your gift from God.
Have you discovered your gift?
Do you think it is too small for God to use?
Are you prepared to harness the little God has placed in your hands? There is a price to pay, to stand before the King.

However small your gifts, do you intend to multiply it?
Do you squander it because you think it is so small and irrelevant?
Do you ignore it because you think that no one cares?
Perhaps, no one would care until they see you in front of the king. So why not begin to prepare for the king's presence!